Technology Across the Curriculum

Technology Across the Curriculum

Activities and Ideas

Marilyn J. Bazeli
Northern Illinois University
De Kalb, Illinois

and

James L. Heintz
Sycamore School District #427
Sycamore, Illinois

1997
Libraries Unlimited, Inc.
And Its Division
Teacher Ideas Press
Englewood, Colorado

Copyright © 1997 Marilyn J. Bazeli and James L. Heintz
All Rights Reserved
Printed in the United States of America

No part of this publication may be reproduced, stored in a retrieval system, or transmitted, in any form or by any means, electronic, mechanical, photocopying, recording, or otherwise, without the prior written permission of the publisher. An exception is made for individual library media specialists and teachers, who may make copies of activity sheets for classroom use in a single school. Other portions of this book (up to 15 pages) may be copied for in-service programs or other educational programs in a single school.

Libraries Unlimited, Inc.
And Its Division
Teacher Ideas Press
P.O. Box 6633
Englewood, CO 80155-6633
1-800-237-6124

Production Editor: Stephen Haenel
Copy Editor: Jason Cook
Interior Design: Michael Florman
Proofreader: Lori Kranz

Library of Congress Cataloging-in-Publication Data

Bazeli, Marilyn J., 1939-
  Technology across the curriculum : activities and ideas /Marilyn
J. Bazeli and James L. Heintz.
     x, 212 p. 22x28 cm.
     Includes bibliographical references and index.
     ISBN 1-56308-444-9
     1. Educational technology--Handbooks, manuals, etc. 2. Media
programs (Education)--Handbooks, manuals, etc. 3. Audio-visual
education--Handbooks, manuals, etc. I. Heintz, James L., 1956-   .
II. Title.
LB1028.3.B395 1997
371.33--dc21   96-45459
                                                             CIP

Contents

Preface vii
Introduction ix

Chapter 1 - Why Engage Students in Technology Productions? 1

Chapter 2 - Video Productions 7
   Biography Book Reports with a Television Twist 12
   Book Discussions 14
   What's Happening in the World? 16
   What's Happening at My School? 18
   Science on Television 20
   Television Documentary 22
   My View of the Story 24
   Create-a-Story 26
   Weekly Spelling Lists 28
   Our School 30
   Selling "Good" Foods 32
   Video Yearbook 34
   Welcome to My Room 36
   Historical Interviews 38
   Living Geometric Shapes 40

Chapter 3 - Photography/Transparency Activities 43
   Pictorial Diaries 48
   Visual Vocabulary 50
   Making Science Visual 52
   Visual Elements in Photos 54
   Mystery Enlargements 56
   History Through Photographs 58
   Visual Weather Records 60
   Rocks and Rock Formations 62
   It's All in the Point of View 64
   Signs of the Seasons 66
   Let's Be Healthy! 68
   Slide Show of Our Community 70
   Effective Transparencies 72
   Projected Constellations 74
   Professional-Quality Drawing with the Overhead Projector 76

Chapter 4 - Audio Productions 79
   Radio Review 84
   Ask and Find Out 86
   Math Jingles 88
   Public Service Announcement 90
   Radio News Update 92
   Halloween Sound Effect Stories 94
   Speaker Stories 96
   "Good Morning" Announcements 98
   One-Minute Reviews 100
   Audio Pen Pals 102
   Story Add-Ons 104
   Sixty-Second Great American 106
   News Flash 108
   Personal Journal 110
   Guess the State 112

Chapter 5 - Computer Activities ... 115
- Draw Me a Story Starter ... 120
- Electronic Notes ... 122
- Computer Tutors ... 124
- Who's Read That? ... 126
- How to Spend a Million Dollars ... 128
- Goal of the Week ... 130
- What's My Grade? ... 132
- Getting to Know You ... 134
- Open House/Conference Notes ... 136
- Computer Pen Pals ... 138
- What's It Like? ... 140
- Spelling Notebook ... 142
- Where to Find It ... 144
- Map the Way ... 146
- Go Find the Grammar ... 148

Chapter 6 - Multimedia Productions ... 151
- Slide/Tape Production: Curricular Areas ... 156
- Slide/Tape Production: Visual Analysis Activity ... 158
- Slide/Tape Production: Special Events ... 160
- Filmstrip/Sound: Old Pictures, New Script ... 162
- Filmstrip/Sound: New Pictures, Old Script ... 164
- Filmstrip/Sound: New Pictures, New Script ... 166
- Slides/Video/Sound: Community, Past and Present ... 168
- Slides/Video/Sound: Family History ... 170
- Slides/Video/Sound: Videotape Slide Productions ... 172
- Video/Sound: Television Without Sound ... 174
- Video/Sound: Television, Critical Thinking, and Sequence ... 176
- Video/Sound/Graphics: Produce an Instructional Video ... 178
- Videodisc: Classroom Movie Critics ... 180
- Videodisc: Problem-Solving Skills ... 182
- Videodisc: Analyze Characters ... 184

Appendix A - Evaluation Sheets ... 187
- How Was My Report? ... 189
- How Was My Presentation? ... 190
- Portfolio Presentation Evaluation Sheet ... 191
- Portfolio Project Evaluation Sheet ... 192
- Portfolio Project Evaluation Sheet ... 193
- Project Evaluation Sheet ... 194
- Assessment for Student Participation ... 195
- Observation of Class Development over Time ... 196
- Creative Choices Assessment ... 197

Appendix B - Scriptwriting Guidelines ... 199
- Scriptwriting Guidelines ... 201
- Dialog Guide ... 202
- Script Guide Sheet ... 203

Appendix C - Extra Equipment and Video Editing ... 204
Appendix D - Classroom Management Tips ... 206
Resources: Media Production Books for Teachers ... 207
Skill Areas Index ... 209
Author/Title/Subject Index ... 211

Preface

The focus of this book is on curricular applications of student media productions, not on specific equipment or production techniques. Familiar media have been selected for these productions so that students are not overwhelmed by the medium itself and are free to focus on the curricular applications as they engage themselves in active, participatory, real-life learning. The simple media used in these activities can easily be replaced by more sophisticated media, if available. The type of media is not the important thing; the important thing is what teachers and students do with various media to make them part of learning.

Students, engaging in these activities, will gain critical-thinking and problem-solving skills necessary to analyze and use media of the information age. Teachers will find this book an invaluable resource for engaging their students in cooperative, creative, integrated, and authentic learning experiences.

Introduction

Many teachers want to use media technology to add a new dimension to classroom learning. However, ideas for such activities are difficult to find. This book offers an exciting, comprehensive collection of teacher-tested classroom activities that incorporate the use of familiar technologies. Using technology enhances classroom activities and provides superb motivation for children of all ages, especially when students are actively involved in media productions. This book is structured for the teacher who has a fundamental understanding of media technology; the teacher with more advanced abilities will find it easy to expand the activities provided here.

The activities cover a wide variety of integrated curriculum areas. The book is divided into the following media categories: video, photography/transparency, audio, computer, and multimedia. Each category contains 15 different activities tested in real classroom situations. Each activity actively engages students in the process of media production for a particular purpose, providing authentic learning experiences. Familiar media have been selected so that the focus is not on learning new production skills but rather on curricular applications, to help students learn. Professional quality of the final production is not the goal in this book (see Appendix E for a listing of selected books on media production); the goal is to involve students in their own learning through their analysis and production of familiar media, integrating cooperative learning, critical thinking, and problem solving.

The outstanding feature of this book is the presentation of creative uses for technologies relative to specific areas of the curriculum, in a familiar format. Each activity includes an objective, an overview of the activity, skill areas that are addressed, a materials checklist, adaptive ideas, a step-by-step procedure guideline, evaluation techniques, and a place for your own ideas and comments. Also included are appendixes providing additional resources for teachers, such as reproducible sheets that can be used with a variety of activities, specialized guidelines and tips, and a list of print resources.

How to Use This Book

Each set of activity sheets should be used as a working document, and should serve as a guide for the entire lesson. The teacher will want to refer to each section during the implementation of the activity.

The **Objective** gives the purpose and goal for the activity. This objective should be stated in class initially and reviewed often as the lesson develops to keep the focus of the activity on track.

The **Overview** provides the teacher with a summary of the activity and student involvement.

Integration of technology into curriculum areas is an important feature of this book. The **Skill Areas** for each activity are listed to demonstrate this integration. Teachers will easily notice that each activity can be applied to many curricular areas; thus, time to complete the activity can be allowed, and thematic lesson planning is possible.

Preparation for the activity is critical. Having all the correct equipment assembled and prepared saves time and prevents complications. The **Materials Checklist** provides a complete list of the equipment necessary to perform the activity.

Because this book is designed for teachers at various grade levels, **Adaptive Ideas** are included. Here, teachers are provided with suggestions to vary the activity for different age groups, and adapt the activity to fit unique instructional situations.

The step-by-step **Procedures** will guide the teacher through the activity in an organized manner. The procedures section of each activity is a guide that can be expanded or modified. An individual class's ability range should dictate the expansion or reduction of the activity.

A number of **Evaluation** ideas are included to offer a variety of assessment techniques. The materials produced can be a wonderful addition to student portfolios, or can be used as part of a grading system. Reflective assessment is an important possibility; as students work on projects, teachers are able to observe and reflect upon the progress of students in many areas, including academic and developmental aspects. Thus, both traditional and nontraditional assessment methods can be used.

A unique feature of this book is the area provided for teachers to record their observations and thoughts related to each activity. Teachers should record the date the project was started, any concerns or problems that developed, and positive outcomes. This will serve as a future reference for each teacher as he/she implements the activity again.

This book is designed by teachers for teachers. The activities add excitement to many curriculum areas. It is hoped that this book will serve as a resource for teachers as they involve students, both actively and creatively, in their own learning. The activities described here not only provide ideas to integrate technology; more importantly, they provide an avenue for changing what teachers and students do in the classroom, so that technology becomes part of the learning process.

Chapter 1

Why Engage Students in Technology Productions?

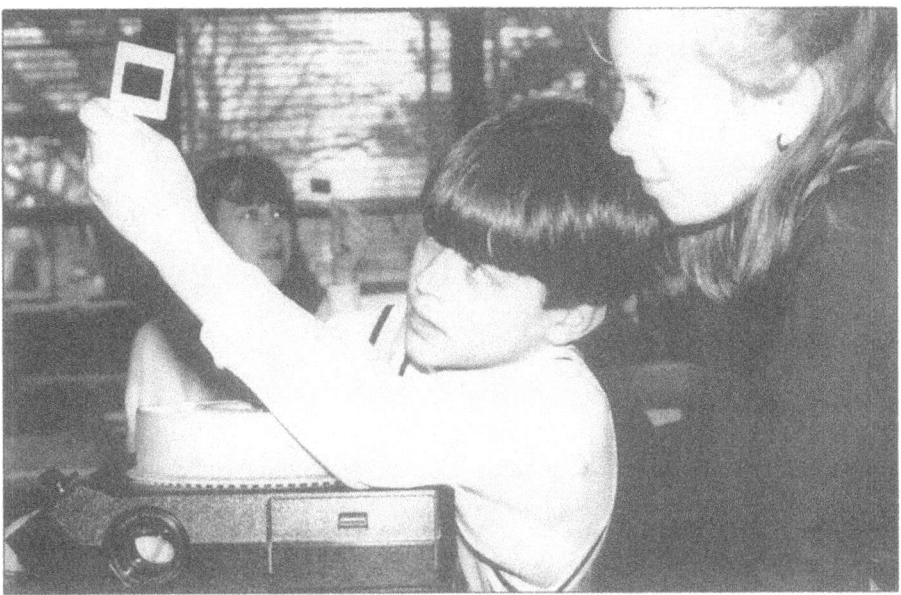

WHY WOULD GOOD TEACHERS want to integrate technology production activities into their classroom plans? Isn't it enough to just be dynamic, exciting instructors? Shouldn't teachers be putting their precious time into preparing for class and providing feedback for students via graded papers? Why would teachers want to spend extra time planning student production activities with technology? Isn't the personal interaction gained from a real teacher/student relationship more helpful than a machine/student relationship?

These questions are asked by many educators. They are valid questions that deserve answers. In this chapter, a theoretical rationale for engaging students in technology production activities will be presented, as well as practical answers to these questions.

> *Why will integrating technology production activities into my classroom help my students learn? What is involved in the process of learning?*

One basic element involved in learning is perception. Perception can be defined as the process whereby a person becomes aware of his or her environment through the use of the senses. People learn from what they perceive, and carefully designed visual experiences can influence that learning in a positive way (Kemp and Smellie, 1994).

Communication is another important element involved in learning. Through communication, messages are sent and received. In an instructional situation, the teacher or instructional media sends the message, and the learner receives it. Some method of feedback must be present to determine the perception of the learners. Obviously, different people perceive the world differently, and communicated messages would also be perceived differently. Therefore, feedback from the learners, such as discussion, written work, and demonstration, is necessary to guide and assess their perception of the messages sent. In addition, the learner's experiential background, or "field of experience," must overlap with the content being presented for understanding to occur (Heinich, Molenda, Russell, and Smaldino,

1996). If a message has no relevance or meaning within the student's experiential background, he or she will not be able to decode the message.

A third important element in learning is the application of instructional and learning theories. Many major theories in educational psychology since the mid-twentieth century have had an impact on instructional methods. Three areas of learning have been discussed frequently: the cognitive domain (knowledge, information, and other intellectual skills); the psychomotor domain (physical skills); and the affective domain (attitudes, values, or beliefs). Robert Gagne (1985) has identified five categories of learning: motor skills; attitudes (values, social norms, moral positions); verbal information (basic names, dates, definitions, organized bodies of knowledge); intellectual skills (learning how to use verbal information, higher-order thinking skills); and cognitive strategies (developing one's own patterns and strategies to remember and think).

Within these frameworks of the areas of learning, many psychologists have investigated how we learn and what teaching strategies are effective. A summary of some of the elements is presented here for review. Read them with technology production activities in mind.

1. Individual differences: Different people learn differently, and thus many types of learning experiences should be provided. Gardner's theory of multiple intelligences (1993) implies that curricular activities should be designed to engage students in varied opportunities to favor those different learning styles.

2. Motivation: Learners need to be involved in a meaningful way with the instructional situation.

3. Learning objectives: Instructors certainly need to know their objectives before a lesson is presented, but learners also need to know what is expected and what the outcome should be.

4. Organization of content: For higher levels of learning to occur (such as analysis, problem solving, or evaluation), content must be organized or structured in such a way that the learner can logically make sense of and remember the content.

5. Participation: Learning requires activity of some kind (either mental or physical), but active, physical participation in the learning process has proven to be the most effective way to promote understanding and retention of the content being presented. Through active participation, the emotions of the learner

are also engaged, which further influences the long-term retention of the content.

6. Practice and repetition: Knowledge needs to be used and repeated in different contexts for long-term memory retention to occur.

7. Feedback: Learners need to be informed of their progress frequently, both for corrective purposes and for reinforcement and support. This feedback can come from the instructor or from peers. An important part of feedback is to provide encouragement, build confidence, and develop a positive self-concept.

8. Application: Learners need to be able to apply knowledge to other situations and to solve new problems. Sharing and explaining content to others can actively involve learners in transferring and applying their knowledge.

(Bell-Gredler, 1986; Kemp and Smellie, 1994)

How does all of this affect the integration of technology production activities into the curriculum?

Perception involves awareness of the world around us. Communication follows perception, with feedback and experience related to the topic being a necessary part. Learning occurs when perception and communication are present. Using technology provides an effective way to engage learners in the world in which they are familiar, and to actively communicate new knowledge within that world. All students have experiential backgrounds involving some type of media; thus, there is a beginning "field of experience" present for effective communication. Producing media provides many opportunities for feedback, both from instructors (given to students) and from students (evaluation of learning). Thus, implementing technology production into the curriculum offers necessary perceptual and communication experiences to students.

Additionally, implementing technology into the curriculum involves the application of major learning theories and various teaching strategies. In terms of the domains of learning, all three (or five if we refer to Gagne) are integral parts of the students' media productions in the classroom. Cognitive, affective, and psychomotor domains are all active elements in curricular student productions.

The learning and teaching theories, summarized previously, relate directly to integrating technology production within the curriculum:

1. Individual differences: All students, regardless of their interests, abilities, personality, learning style, previous learning, physical disabilities, culture, and so on, can participate in technology production. Indeed, all of these differences would add variety and diversity to the productions. Gardner's seven aspects of intelligence (1993), known as multiple intelligences, could be developed through varied types of media production activities.

2. Motivation: Students are highly motivated to produce materials to be shared with others; thus, they are also motivated to learn the necessary content to create an effective production.

3. Learning objectives: Students and teachers both know very clearly what the expected outcome and learning are with each production activity.

4. Organization of content: Before beginning each activity, the organization and sequence of steps are carefully explained and structured, so that students know how they will be proceeding through the learning experience. The content can be organized in various ways (thematically, whole language, etc.), so that many areas of the curriculum are developed within a specific production activity.

5. Participation: Obviously, each student is actively involved in the production activity, in some capacity. Students would often be working in groups, thus developing cooperative group skills.

6. Practice and repetition: As students are actively involved in each production activity, they are continually repeating and practicing content that has been presented in class, or content that they have researched themselves.

7. Feedback: Students would be constantly involved with other students in giving and receiving feedback, both for suggestions regarding their progress and for encouragement and support. Teachers, too, would be continually offering suggestions, reinforcing learning, and praising good work. The content comprehension demonstrated by the students as they produce media provides a valuable assessment tool for teachers.

8. Application: When students are involved in a production activity, they are demonstrating to others their knowledge of the content, and are actively applying their knowledge to a new situation—the production itself.

> *Why would busy teachers want to take time to integrate technology activities into their classroom? Isn't personal interaction more important?*

To function effectively in our global society, students must learn to be good communicators and problem-solvers. They need to progress beyond the lower-level thinking skills such as knowledge and comprehension, to higher-level thinking skills such as critical thinking, analysis, synthesis, and problem solving. How can teachers provide an opportunity for students to develop critical-thinking skills? Further, how can teachers motivate students to want to develop thinking skills?

Our world is becoming more and more visual. Visuals are present everywhere, from T-shirts to bumper stickers. The invention and widespread use of television have added to the multitude of visual messages people receive every day. We depend more and more on visual news reports than on newspapers for our information about the world. Politicians study the effect of their visual representation on the voters. Children find it harder and harder to determine the difference between fantasy seen on television and real-world situations. Violence seen on television seems to be a real-world perception of reality for many children. Do we want our students to be able to apply critical-viewing and critical-thinking skills to all of the many visuals they see? Do we want them to be active instead of passive viewers?

Helping students to gain visual literacy skills can provide answers to many of these questions. Visual literacy can be defined as the ability to interpret and process visual messages, to understand the content of the visuals, and to create effective visuals. Thus, visual literacy involves visual/critical thinking and problem solving as well as active participation in analyzing and producing visuals. Visual literacy is quickly becoming as necessary as verbal literacy. Engaging students in the production of many kinds of visuals provides them with many opportunities to analyze visuals and apply problem-solving and critical-thinking skills to real production situations with which they are involved. As students produce photographs, transparencies, videos, or multimedia packages, they are learning to analyze and think critically about visuals. Do we think it is important for students to learn about techniques of visual production that can influence viewers' thinking? Do we want students to develop visual literacy skills?

Computers are everywhere, and are viewed by many to be highly intelligent and all-knowing. Children are heavily involved in pre-programmed activities on the computer, and thus develop the attitude that the computer is in control. Should we remain complacent with this attitude in students, that a computer cannot be controlled, that it has superior knowledge, or do we want students to view a computer as a tool to help them learn?

Talk shows on radio and lyrics to popular songs convey many auditory messages to people. These and other auditory communications reach young people, but their perception of what they hear may not be what we would like it to be. What are students learning from auditory messages? Do we want them to believe everything they hear? Do we want to help students become discriminating and thoughtful listeners? Do we think it is important for students to learn about techniques of production to influence listeners?

Teachers seem to have less and less time for teaching and planning. Involving students in researching, planning, producing, and evaluating projects can relieve these time problems for teachers. Planning becomes a collaborative activity, with both students and teacher involved in setting up specific lesson plans. Students also share in the evaluation process; as a result, the students' motivation to excel is often greater than it would be by simply turning in a paper for the teacher to grade. Thus, a teacher's time for planning and feedback can actually be shared with students, allowing added opportunity for personal involvement.

It is extremely important for students in schools to become actively involved in media production. As students produce various types of media, they not only learn the content being presented, but they also learn to be critical thinkers, especially regarding what they see and hear—an essential skill in today's world.

Students who are involved in production activities develop cooperative skills and communication skills. Students are constantly involved in developing interpersonal skills. The teacher is also involved personally with the students, often on a one-to-one basis, as they develop plans and complete the production activity. Students must find ways to solve planning and production problems, thus developing their problem-solving abilities in a real-world setting.

Yes, teachers should be exciting and dynamic, and the personal interaction between teacher and student is extremely important! Our goal in education should be to instill a love for learning within our students, to encourage lifelong learning, and to develop knowledgeable and responsible adults who are able to cope with a visual information age. One way to do this is to change what we do in the classroom—engage students in planning and becoming actively involved in their learning experiences. Technology productions by students within the classroom curriculum, along with enthusiastic teachers, can help to accomplish those goals.

References

Bell-Gredler, M. E. 1986. *Learning and instruction: Theory into practice.* New York: Macmillan.

Gagne, R. 1985. *The conditions of learning.* New York: Holt, Rinehart, and Winston.

Gardner, Howard. 1993. *Multiple intelligences: The theory in practice.* New York: Basic Books.

Heinich, R., M. Molenda, J. D. Russell, and S. Smaldino. 1996. *Instructional media and technologies for learning.* Englewood Cliffs, NJ: Prentice-Hall.

Kemp, J., and D. Smellie. 1994. *Planning, producing, and using instructional technologies.* New York: HarperCollins.

Chapter 2
Video Productions

TEACHERS HAVE SUCCESSFULLY introduced and used videotapes and television in their classroom as instructional tools. The properties of video to provide real-life, action visuals make video and films effective classroom tools. When used effectively, video and film can go a long way toward reaching students and getting them involved in and excited about learning. Students can be transported to other worlds, experience other cultures, witness volcanoes exploding, see scientific experiments performed by real scientists, observe changes through the use of slow motion or high-speed photography, and so on. Additionally, and probably most importantly, students learn more and remember more when they see it as well as hear it. The British Audiovisual Association (1983) found that we receive 75 percent of what we learn through sight and 13 percent through hearing (6 percent through touch, 3 percent through taste and smell). The British study also revealed that we retain 20 percent of what we hear, 30 percent of what we see, and 50 percent of what we see *and* hear.

However, students already watch many hours of television outside of school, and even though much of it is for entertainment rather than educational purposes, many teachers are reluctant to add more hours of television to a student's day. One way to provide learning experiences utilizing television is to involve students actively with television by using critical-viewing activities to analyze and produce television programs themselves.

Critical-viewing involves the process of applying problem solving and critical thinking to visual media. Singer, Zuckerman, and Singer (1980) found in an experimental research study that instruction about television aids in developing critical-viewing skills in third-, fourth-, and fifth-grade students.

Considine and Haley (1992) wrote that "our willingness to accept visual representations as accurate reflections of reality is evident in expressions such as 'the camera never lies,' 'seeing is believing,' and 'what you see is what you get' " (p. 18). However, without critical-thinking and critical-viewing skills, students seldom understand what they see, and tend to accept all they see as fact.

Visual competency requires that students have the ability to intelligently send as well as receive visually based communication. Producing television programs has been shown to be effective in developing critical-viewing and -thinking skills in students. Saxton (1988) wrote that instruction and practice in the use of television cameras help children to distinguish fact from fantasy (special effects, etc.), which they see on regular television productions.

By actively involving students in producing television programs, students come to understand the language and symbol system of television, and come to understand communication on many levels (Adams and Hamm, 1987). As students become involved in controlling and producing television, they develop skills to critically evaluate what they see on television.

Though television production skills are not the focus of this book, certain basic production skills should be presented and discussed with students. See the sidebar "Basic Television Production Skills."

Student television productions in various curricular areas not only aid in developing the skill of analyzing visuals and thinking critically, but also aid in cognitive development within the specific curricular areas. As students think about what to present visually and auditorially in their television production, they also are developing comprehension and analysis skills regarding the topic.

In addition, students enjoy the entire process of videotaping projects in the classroom. The idea that the end-product of their hard work will be recorded for later viewing brings a great excitement to the learning process. Further, students feel more accountable for the project when they know they will be videotaped. The motivational value of the camcorder as a technology tool to aid in the learning process is substantial.

The audio and visual feedback inherent in videotape offers an excellent opportunity for portfolio assessment and as a measure of development for students as they continue through school. In addition, students can increase their own self-awareness and self-efficacy by observing their performances over time to see growth in confidence, physical appearance, presentation skills, and curricular knowledge.

This chapter contains introductory ideas for critical-thinking development involving student television production in various curricular areas. As you, the instructor, begin to use television production as a tool for developing thinking in your students, within a particular curricular area, many ideas will evolve in your mind and in students' minds. To assist you in evolving these ideas for implementing television production into your classroom curricular areas, a blank page for your comments follows this chapter.

Basic Television Production Skills

1. Point the camera away from sun or lights to avoid permanent damage to the camera.

2. Observe the "rule of thirds" for production of all visuals: The weakest visual space is dead center. The strongest visual locations are at the points where the lines intersect. Basically, use the top third of the viewing area.

3. Check background for distractors.

4. Allow space for people to walk in or out of frame.

5. Use tripod whenever possible. Always check for tight attachments.

6. Vary shots to add interest; however, don't overdo changing types of shots. Some types of shots include:

- close-up: conveys emotions, or how to do something.
- long shot: shows location.
- high-angle shot: the camera looks down on the subject; this creates the illusion that the subject is small, inferior, or lonely.
- low-angle shot: the camera is placed below the subject; this makes the subject appear stronger and gives the illusion that the subject is superior.

7. Make all camera moves slowly. For pans, tilts, and zooms, start the motion and continue; don't start, stop, and start again.

8. Special effects can get boring quickly. Don't overdo them.

Extracurricular Event—"Video Night"

A video night was held for students, parents, friends, and relatives to showcase three videotapes the students had produced. Parent volunteers made popcorn and served juice as more than 90 people (for a class of 25 students) attended the evening festivities. The children were proud of their performances and achievements, and excited about sharing their productions with their parents, family, and friends. The adults expressed only positive comments and greatly appreciated the efforts of the students in their productions and the learning that was demonstrated. The evening was an overwhelming success!

References

Adams, D., and M. Hamm. 1987. Teaching students critical viewing skills. *Curriculum Review* 16, no. 3: 29–32.

British Audiovisual Association. 1983. Report, as quoted in *InteractiveVideo*, edited by Eric Parsloe and researched by Signe Hoffos and the EPIC Team. Cheshire, U.K.: Sigma Technical Press.

Considine, D., and Gail Haley. 1992. *Visual messages: Integrating imagery into instruction.* Englewood, CO: Teacher Ideas Press.

Saxton, B. 1988. VCR visual techniques for fifth- and sixth-graders—More than turning it on! In *Visual literacy in life and learning: Readings from the 19th Annual Conference of the International Visual Literacy Association* (pp. 421–46), edited by R. Braden, B. Braden, D. Beauchamp, and L. Miller. Blacksburg: Virginia Tech University.

Singer, D., D. Zuckerman, and J. Singer. 1980. Helping elementary school children learn about TV. *Journal of Communication* 30, no. 3 (Summer): 84–93.

More Ideas

Curricular Areas　　　　　　　　　　**Production Ideas**

From *Technology Across the Curriculum.* © 1997. Marilyn J. Bazeli and James L. Heintz. Teacher Ideas Press. (800) 237-6124.

Activities

Biography Book Reports with a Television Twist

Objective
Students present reports as if they were the person in the biography.

Overview
Motivating students to read books is sometimes a difficult task. This activity is designed to encourage students to read and then report on their book in a creative way. The videotaped reports could be housed in the school library for other students to view, and thus motivate others to read the book.

Skill Areas
Reading, English, Oral Communication

Materials Checklist
☐ Video camera

Adaptive Ideas
Students of all ages can participate in this activity. Young children can prepare shorter reports, while older children should be encouraged to present more thorough character analyses. For all ages of students, the process of preparing and presenting facts and perceptions about a book they read has great value in terms of comprehension and interpretation of the written word. The depth of perception and interpretation will vary with students' abilities.

Procedures
1. Each student selects a biography (or autobiography) to read.
2. After reading the book, each student prepares a report about the book as if he or she were the person about whom the story was written. The story should be told in the first person.
3. The student should attempt to dress as the person in his or her book would be dressed, and any other props lending to the appearance of the person should be added. For example, a biography of Michael Jordan would involve a Bulls uniform or T-shirt, and perhaps a prop of a basketball.
4. The student practices his or her report in terms of voice, accent, mannerisms, and so on, to depict the character he or she is assuming.
5. Videotape each student's report, complete with costumes and props.
6. Share the finished tapes with other classes or with individual students in a library setting.

From *Technology Across the Curriculum.* © 1997. Marilyn J. Bazeli and James L. Heintz. Teacher Ideas Press. (800) 237-6124.

Evaluation

Select an appropriate evaluation form provided in appendix A.

For Portfolios:

☐ Photocopy the written report of each student.

☐ Make a copy of the videotaped presentation of each student.

Teacher's Notes

Dates: _____

Books used: _____

Remarks: _____

_____

_____

_____

_____

_____

From *Technology Across the Curriculum.* © 1997. Marilyn J. Bazeli and James L. Heintz. Teacher Ideas Press. (800) 237-6124.

14 / Chapter 2: Video Productions

Book Discussions

Objective
Two or three students read and report on the same book, in a group-discussion forum.

Overview
Two or three students each read the same book. The students prepare a group discussion of the book, stating things they liked or disliked about the book, parts of the story they found most exciting or interesting, characters they liked or disliked and why, and so on. Students will have different opinions, and an interesting discussion should result (a forum similar to Siskel and Ebert's "reviews" of motion pictures).

Skill Areas
Reading, English, Oral Presentation, Cooperative Group Work

Materials Checklist
- ☐ Video camera
- ☐ Optional: Tape player (for music at beginning and end)

Adaptive Ideas
Students of all ages can participate in this activity. The length, depth, and quality of the planned discussion will vary with the ability and age of the students.

Procedures
1. Students, in groups of two or three, select a book that each student in the group will read (any genre will work for this activity).
2. After reading the book, students individually decide such things as: what they liked/disliked about the book, what characters they liked, what were the most exciting or interesting parts of the book, and so on.
3. Students within each group share their thoughts and opinions about the book and organize these into a discussion format.
4. Students practice the formal book discussion, making eye contact with each other as they discuss their opinions.
5. Videotape the book discussions. Remind students to look at each other and not at the camera when sharing their opinions. Optional: Present the discussion as a television program, with off-camera announcing, music, title screens, introduction of program and "stars," closing announcements and end credits, and so on.
6. Share the videotaped discussions with other classes or store them in the library for individual students to view when deciding upon a book to read (the videotapes should be filed according to genre for easy access by teachers and students).

From *Technology Across the Curriculum.* © 1997. Marilyn J. Bazeli and James L. Heintz. Teacher Ideas Press. (800) 237-6124.

Evaluation

Select an appropriate evaluation form provided in appendix A. Students could also be evaluated in terms of voice, expression, overall presentation, and so on.

For Portfolios:

☐ Photocopy the written outline of discussion by each student.

☐ Make a copy of the videotaped discussion of each student group.

Teacher's Notes

Dates: _____

Books discussed: _____

Remarks: _____

_____

_____

_____

_____

_____

16 / Chapter 2: Video Productions

What's Happening in the World?

Objective
Students research, write, and deliver a news broadcast containing world news, local news, and sports news.

Overview
It is sometimes difficult to engage students in the investigation of current events. With this activity, students research major news events in three areas: world, local, and sports. Students compile their information into scripts of designated length. They practice their news broadcasts and then deliver them as student-produced videotaped news programs.

Skill Areas
Social Studies, English, Reading, Research, Oral Presentation

Materials Checklist
- ☐ Newspapers
- ☐ News magazines
- ☐ Video camera
- ☐ Optional: Tape player (for music at beginning and end)
- ☐ Optional: Internet connection to newspapers/news reports

Adaptive Ideas
Students of all ages can participate in this activity. The detail and depth of the news investigation will vary depending upon the grade level of the students involved.

Procedures
1. Gather newspapers and news magazines for students.
2. Divide students into news teams of six students.
3. Each team selects one or two current news stories in each of the following categories: world, local, and sports. One or two students select a category, read about the selected stories in that category, and write a summary of the stories for the reporter to deliver. Each category will be researched by one or two students in the group.
4. Each team decides the role of each member: world news reporter, local news reporter, sports reporter, camera person, set designer, special effects (music, off-camera announcing, etc.).
5. Each team member practices his or her role.
6. Students videotape their news broadcasts and then show them to the entire class.

From *Technology Across the Curriculum.* © 1997. Marilyn J. Bazeli and James L. Heintz. Teacher Ideas Press. (800) 237-6124.

Evaluation

Select an appropriate evaluation form provided in appendix A.

For Portfolios:

☐ Photocopy the completed scripts.

☐ Make copies of students' video performances.

Teacher's Notes

Dates: _____

Stories Covered: _____

Remarks: _____

_____

_____

_____

_____

_____

From *Technology Across the Curriculum.* © 1997. Marilyn J. Bazeli and James L. Heintz. Teacher Ideas Press. (800) 237-6124.

What's Happening at My School?

Objective
Students discover, write, and report news of classroom events or schoolwide events within their school environment.

Overview
Often, students and teachers within one school community are not aware of events taking place in the various classrooms. This activity motivates students to interview the teachers and other students within the school community. Students write scripts reporting school events, practice their scripts, and deliver them as student-produced videotaped school news programs.

Skill Areas
English, Reading, Oral Presentation, Communication/Interviewing

Materials Checklist
- ☐ Video camera
- ☐ Optional: Tape recorder (used during interviews, or for music at beginning and end)

Adaptive Ideas
Students of all ages can participate in this activity. The degree to which information about school/classroom events is discovered and reported will vary with the grade level of the students involved. The use of the camcorder and/or tape recorder for segments of the production will be more extensive with older students.

Procedures
1. Divide students into news teams of six students.
2. Assign to each team a component of the school (grade level, curricular area, administrative office, etc.). Each team interviews people within the assigned component to find news of events or happenings within that component. (Students might wish to use tape recorders to help them remember the responses. Younger students, especially, who might have trouble writing down responses, should use this technique.)
3. Each team member writes a script for one segment of the news for the assigned school component. (This may be done in pairs.)
4. Each team decides the role of each member: three reporters, a camera person, set designer, special effects (music, off-camera announcing, etc.).
5. Each team member practices his or her role.
6. Students videotape their news broadcasts. (For older students, an on-camera interview with some other person within the school could be incorporated into the news report. This would involve somewhat advanced interviewing skills. Younger students can incorporate a short audio-recorded interview.)

From *Technology Across the Curriculum.* © 1997. Marilyn J. Bazeli and James L. Heintz. Teacher Ideas Press. (800) 237-6124.

7. Share the videotaped news programs with the entire school, show them at parent meetings, and/or present them at community events.

Evaluation

Select an appropriate evaluation form provided in appendix A.

For Portfolios:

☐ Photocopy the scripts.

☐ Make copies of individual on-camera student performances.

Teacher's Notes

Dates: _____

School components covered: _____

Remarks: _____

_____

_____

_____

_____

_____

From *Technology Across the Curriculum*. © 1997. Marilyn J. Bazeli and James L. Heintz. Teacher Ideas Press. (800) 237-6124.

Science on Television

Objective
Students prepare and present a science experiment or activity to accompany a unit of science being investigated by the class.

Overview
Science experiments are an effective discovery technique; however, students are not always clear in their procedures or explanation of steps. This activity helps students think through experiments and activities carefully and present them for video production.

Skill Areas
Science, Research, English, Oral Presentation

Materials Checklist
- ☐ Video camera
- ☐ Appropriate science equipment

Adaptive Ideas
This is primarily an upper-grade activity; however, young children can perform and explain simple science activities. An alternate idea for using the videotaped experiment: Show the experiment *without using sound*. Ask the students for ideas about what is happening and why. This is a good starting point for forming hypotheses and application of critical-thinking skills.

Procedures
1. Students, in groups or individually, research and select an activity or experiment pertaining to the topic being studied in class (students can consult teachers as a resource).
2. Students gather materials necessary for the chosen activity or experiment.
3. Students try the activity or experiment themselves to determine the steps involved and results of these steps.
4. Students prepare a written procedure for the activity or experiment, with a full explanation of each procedure. The results of the activity or experiment, with scientifically based evaluation of these results, should be included.
5. Students practice the activity/experiment using the accompanying script that they have written.
6. Videotape the entire activity or experiment. Optional: Present the experiment as a television science show, complete with title, music, and announcing, similar to a "Mr. Wizard" show—this might be done with one student on camera, or the students might present the activity/experiment in groups, with one student playing the role of the scientist, and the others the learners. As previously mentioned, the segment of an experiment where something is visibly occurring might be shown to the class *without sound* to elicit thinking and hypothesis-forming on the part of the students in the class (example: a can crushing, with no audio explanation that air pressure is causing this to occur).

From *Technology Across the Curriculum.* © 1997. Marilyn J. Bazeli and James L. Heintz. Teacher Ideas Press. (800) 237-6124.

Evaluation

Select an appropriate evaluation form provided in appendix A.

For Portfolios:

☐ Photocopy the written procedures and explanations.

☐ Make a copy of the videotaped presentations.

Teacher's Notes

Dates: _____

Experiment: _____

Science topic area: _____

Remarks: _____

_____

_____

_____

_____

From *Technology Across the Curriculum.* © 1997. Marilyn J. Bazeli and James L. Heintz. Teacher Ideas Press. (800) 237-6124.

Television Documentary

Objective

Students plan and produce a short television program, in documentary form, about some aspect of a topic being studied in class. (A documentary can be defined as a program format documenting a real event rather than creating a scripted one.)

Overview

Students work in groups of three to four students and select a particular aspect, or subtopic, of a current classroom topic that they want to investigate. Students find pertinent information about that subtopic and then go into the community to videotape a documentation of their investigation. For example, if the class is studying plants, students might select wildflowers of their geographic area as a subtopic to investigate. They would research information and pictures of the common wildflowers so that they would be able to identify them. Next, students would document on videotape a trip through a wooded area containing varieties of wildflowers. If the class is studying the community as a social studies topic, students might select a subtopic such as agriculture, architecture, or businesses, research that subtopic, and then videotape real events, tours, or interviews within that subtopic.

Skill Areas

All Curricular Areas, Cooperative Group Work, Research

Materials Checklist

☐ Reference books pertaining to topic
☐ Video camera

Adaptive Ideas

Young children will need to have an adult accompany them to do the videotaping. Older children, with proper instruction, could possibly do the videotaping themselves. Because of the mobility necessary for this project, extra production assistance from an adult and small camcorders would be helpful.

Procedures

1. Students in groups of two to four select a subtopic they want to investigate.
2. Students research the subtopic and record information found.
3. The teacher assists the students in finding locations and/or resource people within the community to illustrate the subtopic they are investigating (example: locate types of architecture, woodland areas, businesses, subject experts to visit/interview, etc.).
4. Students plan a trip to the chosen locations and decide upon and list things at these locations to document in their video to provide a variety of visual experiences.

From *Technology Across the Curriculum.* © 1997. Marilyn J. Bazeli and James L. Heintz. Teacher Ideas Press. (800) 237-6124.

5. Each group writes a script for their video.
6. Students (accompanied by adult) travel to the designated locations to videotape the documentary of their subtopic.
7. Students share the finished documentaries with the class. Finished documentaries may also be shown at community events or parent meetings—the documentaries can be a learning experience for the community as well.

Evaluation

Select an appropriate evaluation form provided in appendix A.

For Portfolios:

☐ Photocopy students' planning sheets and scripts.

☐ Make copies of the documentaries.

Teacher's Notes

Dates: _____

Classroom topic involved: _____

Subtopics investigated by students: _____

Locations in community: _____

Adult helpers: _____

Remarks: _____

_____

_____

_____

From *Technology Across the Curriculum.* © 1997. Marilyn J. Bazeli and James L. Heintz. Teacher Ideas Press. (800) 237-6124.

24 / Chapter 2: Video Productions

My View of the Story

Objective
Each student gives a book report from the character's point of view.

Overview
Each student reads a book with a well-defined character. Each student prepares an oral report from the character's point of view. Voice, costume, and acting should be incorporated into the report.

Skill Areas
Reading, Point of View, Oral Communication

Materials Checklist
- ☐ Video camera
- ☐ Books with well-defined characters
- ☐ Costumes

Adaptive Ideas
Pairs of students might read the same book and give a report as two characters interacting.

Procedures
1. Students select and read a book with a well-defined character.
2. Each student prepares a two- to three-minute book report from the character's point of view.
3. Students prepare costumes and practice speaking and acting appropriately for the character.
4. Students prepare any necessary props to enhance the report.
5. Videotape the presentations.

From *Technology Across the Curriculum.* © 1997. Marilyn J. Bazeli and James L. Heintz. Teacher Ideas Press. (800) 237-6124.

Evaluation

Select an appropriate evaluation form provided in appendix A.

For Portfolios:

☐ Make a copy of the videotaped presentation of each student.

Teacher's Notes

Dates: _____

Types of books read: _____

Costuming ideas: _____

Remarks: _____

_____

_____

_____

_____

From *Technology Across the Curriculum*. © 1997. Marilyn J. Bazeli and James L. Heintz. Teacher Ideas Press. (800) 237-6124.

Create-a-Story

Objective
Students write, illustrate, and record an original story on videotape.

Overview
Students write an original story, prepare illustrations for the story, and videotape the story as a sequence of illustrations held in front of the camera with accompanying narration.

Skill Areas
Creative Writing, Art, Oral Communication

Materials Checklist
- ☐ Video camera
- ☐ Drawing paper
- ☐ Crayons or markers

Adaptive Ideas
Younger students should read a story from a book while the illustrations are held in front of the video camera by a helper. Older students might videotape stories that younger children will enjoy. Students might devote extra time to work on speaking dynamics.

Procedures
1. Each student writes an original story (this can be accomplished in small groups).
2. Students create several illustrations for their stories (the number of illustrations depends on the length of the story and the age and ability of the student).
3. Set up the video camera so the illustration is the entire focus of the picture.
4. The story is read aloud while the illustrations are slowly changed (a stand is helpful for changing the illustrations).
5. Show the videotapes to the class or to other grades.

From *Technology Across the Curriculum.* © 1997. Marilyn J. Bazeli and James L. Heintz. Teacher Ideas Press. (800) 237-6124.

Evaluation

Stories should be evaluated based on the writing and the illustrations, as well as content and mechanics. The art instructor might wish to play a role in the creation and evaluation of the illustrations. The video performance should be evaluated on the dynamics of the presenter in the story.

For Portfolios:

☐ Photocopy the story and illustrations of each student.

☐ Make a copy of the videotaped presentation of each student.

Teacher's Notes

Dates: _____

Story topics: _____

Type of illustrations used: _____

Uses of the stories: _____

Remarks: _____

_____

_____

_____

From *Technology Across the Curriculum.* © 1997. Marilyn J. Bazeli and James L. Heintz. Teacher Ideas Press. (800) 237-6124.

Weekly Spelling Lists

Objective
Students present weekly spelling lists for videotaping.

Overview
Weekly spelling lists are videotaped to be used for final tests. Readers of the weekly lists might include the teacher, students, former students of the school, the principal, community members, or parents.

Skill Area
Spelling

Materials Checklist
- ☐ Video camera
- ☐ Spelling lists
- ☐ Practice sentences
- ☐ Optional: Microphone

Adaptive Ideas
The videotaping of spelling lists can be adapted to other curricular areas, such as science or social studies vocabulary or math facts.

Procedures
1. Set up the video camera for an eye-pleasing background.
2. Prepare spelling lists and lists of practice sentences (if possible, allow rehearsal time for the performers).
3. Videotape the spelling lists. Make sure the lists are read with a proper pause interval between the words (if performers do read too fast, the pause button on the VCR can be used during the viewing). Make sure the performer gives his or her name and perhaps a few words of encouragement to personalize the lesson. If possible, record several lists at each setup time.

From *Technology Across the Curriculum.* © 1997. Marilyn J. Bazeli and James L. Heintz. Teacher Ideas Press. (800) 237-6124.

Evaluation

The teacher should make sure there are no distractions while the list is presented and should carefully monitor student reaction to the prerecorded list. Ask for students' opinions on the format after each lesson is presented.

Teacher's Notes

Dates: _____

Setup problems: _____

Presenters: _____

Lists used: _____

Remarks: _____

_____

_____

_____

From *Technology Across the Curriculum.* © 1997. Marilyn J. Bazeli and James L. Heintz. Teacher Ideas Press. (800) 237-6124.

Our School

Objective
Students create a promotional videotape describing their school.

Overview
Students "partition" their school for investigation. All specific places, such as the office, art room, music room, gym, nurse's office, classrooms, cafeteria, and so on, should be included. The students write a short description of the locations. Students act like news reporters at the location during the taping.

Skill Areas
Written Communication, Oral Communication

Materials Checklist
- ☐ Video camera
- ☐ Microphone

Adaptive Ideas
The topics might center around the community, state, nation, or foreign country. Students might also interview persons responsible for the area of the school described.

Procedures
1. Students partition their school into areas integral to the operation of the school.
2. Students working individually or in small groups write a description of one location. The description should be written in a narrative format.
3. Students rehearse the narrative scripts as if they were reporters on-site.
4. Students videotape each location in sequence on one videotape. (To eliminate editing, plan the sequence in advance.) If possible, students should begin with an overall description of the school, shooting outside to show the front of the school building.
5. Students videotape a conclusion that ties the project together.

Evaluation

Select an appropriate evaluation form provided in appendix A. Show the videotape to other classes, at Parent-Teacher Organization meetings, and to new students.

For Portfolios:

☐ Photocopy each student's written script.

☐ Make a copy of the videotaped presentation of each student.

Teacher's Notes

Dates: _____

Parts of the school: _____

Remarks: _____

_____

_____

_____

_____

_____

From *Technology Across the Curriculum.* © 1997. Marilyn J. Bazeli and James L. Heintz. Teacher Ideas Press. (800) 237-6124.

32 / Chapter 2: Video Productions

Selling "Good" Foods

Objective
Students write a commercial to promote foods that children find less than desirable, such as cauliflower, celery, and spinach.

Overview
Students, working in groups, write a script for a commercial to promote or "sell" a food they find undesirable. Each group researches the benefits of their food. Each group provides the appropriate props for their commercial.

Skill Areas
Health, Science, Research, Creative Writing, Oral Presentation

Materials Checklist
- ☐ Video camera
- ☐ Script Guide Sheet (page 203; duplicate as many as needed)
- ☐ Dialog Guide (page 202)
- ☐ Optional: Stopwatch

Adaptive Ideas
The commercial concept can be adapted to other curricular areas, such as the procedure for long division (math), naming the planets (science), facts about the 50 states (social studies), and so on. To prompt well-prepared and concise commercials, limit the allotted time to 30 or 60 seconds.

Procedures
1. Divide the class into groups and have each group choose an "undesirable" food.
2. Student groups research the food for nutritive benefits, preparation (including ways to make it more appealing), and so on.
3. Each group writes a script for the commercial using the Dialog Guide provided in the appendix. Each speaker and his or her dialog should be listed, along with props necessary to better "sell" the food.
4. Each group prepares their props.
5. Each group rehearses their commercial. If assigning a specific time limit, have the students use a stopwatch.
6. Videotape the commercials.

From *Technology Across the Curriculum.* © 1997. Marilyn J. Bazeli and James L. Heintz. Teacher Ideas Press. (800) 237-6124.

Evaluation

Select an appropriate evaluation form provided in appendix A.

For Portfolios:

☐ Make a copy of the videotaped presentation of each student.

Teacher's Notes

Dates: _____

Food topics: _____

Props used: _____

Remarks: _____

_____

_____

_____

_____

From *Technology Across the Curriculum.* © 1997. Marilyn J. Bazeli and James L. Heintz. Teacher Ideas Press. (800) 237-6124.

Video Yearbook

Objective
Students record the events of the school year on videotape.

Overview
Students prepare a chronological recording of the entire school year. All major events, formal and informal activities, student work, and student interactions are recorded to be retained as a keepsake.

Skill Areas
All curriculum areas.

Materials Checklist
☐ Video camera

Adaptive Ideas
Collect different video clips from student activities. Have a local college or high school video class edit the tape to prepare a 30-minute review of the year.

Procedures
1. Prepare one videotape to be used all year long.
2. Record short video segments of events throughout the entire school year. Events should include the first day of school, field trips, parties, special assemblies, and student projects. Events should include candid shots and students speaking.
3. Have students bring blank videotapes to make copies for a keepsake. The media center director or parents might be willing to assist in creating the copies.

From *Technology Across the Curriculum.* © 1997. Marilyn J. Bazeli and James L. Heintz. Teacher Ideas Press. (800) 237-6124.

Evaluation
Solicit parent and student feedback on the overall value of the keepsake.

Teacher's Notes

Dates: _____

Activities taped: _____

Number of students wanting the keepsake: _____

Remarks: _____

_____

_____

_____

_____

From *Technology Across the Curriculum.* © 1997. Marilyn J. Bazeli and James L. Heintz. Teacher Ideas Press. (800) 237-6124.

Welcome to My Room

Objective
Students prepare videotaped "introductions" for using areas of the classroom, library, lunch room, and so on.

Overview
Students write and present their interpretation on the function of the classroom, how to use the library, lunchroom procedures, and so on.

Skill Areas
Written Communication, Oral Communication

Materials Checklist
☐ Video camera

Adaptive Ideas
Older students might prepare videotapes to be used as a resource to demonstrate how to check out a book, how to take attendance, or how to use an in-class library.

Procedures
1. Divide the class into small groups.
2. Each group selects (or the teacher designates) a section (function) of the classroom or a school procedure.
3. Each group writes a script and decides on the props needed to give a full introduction and explanation of the topic. The group should include as many members of the group in the presentation as possible.
4. Each group rehearses their presentation.
5. Show the videos at an open house or to new students.

From *Technology Across the Curriculum*. © 1997. Marilyn J. Bazeli and James L. Heintz. Teacher Ideas Press. (800) 237-6124.

Evaluation

Select an appropriate evaluation form provided in appendix A.

For Portfolios:

☐ Photocopy the written script of each student.

☐ Make a copy of the videotaped presentation of each student.

Teacher's Notes

Dates: _____

Topics used: _____

_____

_____

_____

_____

_____

_____

From *Technology Across the Curriculum.* © 1997. Marilyn J. Bazeli and James L. Heintz. Teacher Ideas Press. (800) 237-6124.

Historical Interviews

Objective
Students study historical figures and present the information as an interview.

Overview
Pairs of students research a biography of a historical figure, such as Abraham Lincoln, Martin Luther King Jr., Albert Einstein, and so on. Each student pair prepares interview questions and appropriate answers for the historical figure.

Skill Areas
Reading, Research, Writing, Oral Communication, Social Studies, Science

Materials Checklist
- ☐ Video camera
- ☐ Microphone
- ☐ Research materials
- ☐ Costumes

Adaptive Ideas
Older students might research political figures. Students might dress in appropriate costumes to add realism to the project.

Procedures
1. Divide the class into pairs.
2. Each student pair selects a historical figure to research. Select suitable topics from the science or social studies curriculum.
3. Each student pair prepares a series of interview questions that would be appropriate for the historical figure. The questions asked and answered should be based on the research.
4. Using an interview format and a microphone, each student pair presents their historical figure. One student is the interviewer and one plays the role of the historical figure. (Practice using a microphone for the interview format. Remembering to move the microphone back and forth between the interviewer and the personality takes practice.)

From *Technology Across the Curriculum.* © 1997. Marilyn J. Bazeli and James L. Heintz. Teacher Ideas Press. (800) 237-6124.

Evaluation

Select an appropriate evaluation form provided in appendix A.

For Portfolios:

☐ Make a copy of the videotaped presentation of each pair of students.

Teacher's Notes

Dates: _____

Research topics: _____

Costuming ideas: _____

Remarks: _____

_____

_____

_____

_____

From *Technology Across the Curriculum.* © 1997. Marilyn J. Bazeli and James L. Heintz. Teacher Ideas Press. (800) 237-6124.

Living Geometric Shapes

Objective
Student groups demonstrate the number of sides of a given geometric shape by using their bodies.

Overview
Students are given a shape (parallelogram, hexagon, etc.). Students lie down on the ground to create the shape, using one or several members of the group to represent each side of the shape.

Skill Areas
Math, Group Participation, Cooperation Group Work

Materials Checklist
- ☐ Video camera
- ☐ Ladder or access to the top of the school

Adaptive Ideas
Older students might form three-dimensional shapes using people and 2-x-4 pieces of lumber. Younger students might form letters or words as they are called out by the teacher.

Procedures
1. Divide the class into groups of eight.
2. Set up the video camera on a tall ladder or on top of the school building. (Check your school policy before doing this step.)
3. The teacher or student prompter calls out a shape for the group to assemble.
4. The group, using the bodies of the group members, creates the shape by lying on the ground (one student for each side of the shape).
5. The teacher or student prompter calls out another shape and the group forms the shape by adding members or removing members as necessary.
6. Review videotapes with students.

From *Technology Across the Curriculum.* © 1997. Marilyn J. Bazeli and James L. Heintz. Teacher Ideas Press. (800) 237-6124.

Evaluation

In group discussion, use the videotape as the basis to critique completed shapes and to reinforce and review the types of shapes.

Teacher's Notes

Dates: _____

Shapes given: _____

Location of the video camera: _____

Remarks: _____

_____

_____

_____

_____

From *Technology Across the Curriculum.* © 1997. Marilyn J. Bazeli and James L. Heintz. Teacher Ideas Press. (800) 237-6124.

Chapter 3

Photography/Transparency Activities

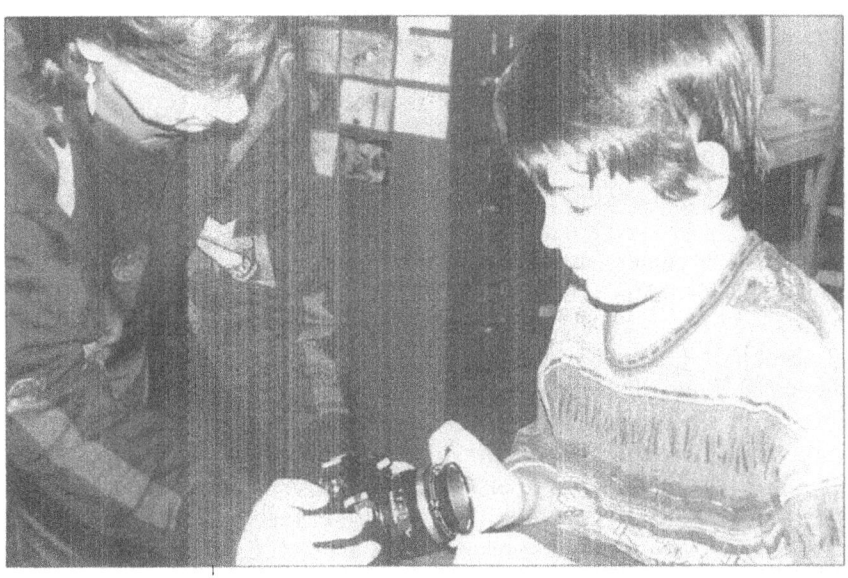

IT HAS LONG BEEN KNOWN that visuals help students learn. In 1657, Johannes Amos Comenius for the first time used visuals in a book for the purpose of enhancing learning, instead of just decorating. Underlying his use of visuals was the idea that we learn through all of our senses, especially through sight. Seeing leads to the creation of a mental image, which in turn leads to understanding. Comenius believed that, while a real object is preferable, visuals in books could be used in place of the real thing to provide interest and concrete referents for learning (Heinich, Molenda, Russell, and Smaldino, 1996). Since then, visuals have been a major part of instruction.

Many writers and researchers have investigated the impact of visuals on learning. Spoehr and Lehmkuhle (1982) studied visual information processing. They suggested that visuals are cognitively processed into long-term memory faster than words, and that visual memory is better (longer lasting and easier to recall) than verbal memory.

Studies regarding the use of visuals in connection with learning style reveal that critical-viewing skills and the use of visuals may involve the use of both right- and left-brain hemispheres (Hanson, Silver, and Strong, 1988). Processing of the visual itself involves the right brain (intuitive, spatial), and the interpretation of the visual involves the left brain (concrete, relational). Because human beings use a mixture of left- and right-brain thinking processes, Lacy (1988) believes that there is a need to promote growth in both hemispheres, the visual as well as the verbal.

Eisner (1982) stated that using visuals to teach visual perception also increases perceptual and cognitive growth. He wrote that the formation of concepts "depends upon the construction of images derived from the material the senses provide" (p. 34).

Joshua Taylor of the National Gallery has stated, "To see is to think" (Lacy, 1988, p. 35). Costa (1985) advocated that "seeing" and thinking should be taught together throughout the curriculum, in relation to content. "Seeing" is the concept of visual literacy, which includes both analysis and production of visuals.

"Pictures can clarify complex ideas, make them easier to remember, and provoke emotional responses" (Heinich, Molenda, Russell, and Smaldino, 1996, p. 64). Visuals play three important roles in learning. They provide: 1) a concrete way to remember new ideas, as well as help attract and keep the attention of the learners; 2) an organized iconic method to help learners understand difficult information, using such forms as diagrams, flowcharts, and timelines; and 3) a different modality, other than verbal, for comprehending new information, using the "visual intelligence" of the learners (Heinich, Molenda, Russell, and Smaldino, 1996).

The Polaroid Company has been very active in promoting the use of photographs to develop thinking and visual literacy skills. They provide teacher workshops and produce frequent newsletters and lesson plans for teachers using photography in the classroom.

Students enjoy using a camera and creating transparencies. As with most student-produced visual activities, students are very motivated to create something they are proud of, especially when they know it will be viewed by others. Further, they feel more accountable for their learning when they know that the completed project will be on display, either in their own classroom or somewhere else.

However, even though much has been written discussing the importance of visuals in the learning process, many teachers still rely upon words as communication vehicles. The purpose of this chapter is to provide ideas for still pictures: photography/transparency production by students, to develop their visual literacy skills and their understanding of subject areas. For ease of use for students, an automatic camera is suggested. Though the materials listed for photography activities are a camera and either slide or print film, a digital camera can easily be substituted, if available. Photographs printed on a color printer or projected from the computer via an LCD panel can also be substituted. Whatever equipment is available, from the simplest to the most sophisticated, it is hoped that the ideas presented here will encourage the use of these media in your classrooms and promote the creation of more ideas. A blank page is provided for you to record your (or students') ideas for future use.

Students will need instruction regarding the operation of the specific camera they will use. This might be a traditional camera (using film) or a digital camera. Before students begin a photography assignment, they should learn some basic guidelines for creating effective photographs. See the sidebar "Basic Photography Guidelines."

In many of the following lessons, a copystand is needed. Copystands are used for photographing pictures in books or magazines as well as two- and three-dimensional objects. The description and diagram of a copystand, and instructions for its use, are provided in appendix C.

Basic Photography Guidelines

1. When deciding what to include in the photograph, be sure to include subjects needed to communicate your intended message.

2. Be careful to look at the areas behind and beside your subject(s). Shiny surfaces or unnecessary objects are distracting.

3. Compose pictures keeping the "Rule of Thirds" in mind. (The Rule of Thirds states that, when the picture area is divided into thirds with both vertical and horizontal lines, the strongest visual locations are at the intersections of the lines.) Thus, the main subject of a photograph should never be in the exact center, nor crowded into a corner.

4. Don't divide the photograph exactly in half. If there is a horizontal line (such as the ocean), or a vertical line (such as a tree), place it off-center.

5. To convey a feeling of depth, place a foreground object at one side to frame the main subject. (For example, for a photograph of the ocean, place a person or beach chair in the foreground, or include an onshore tree at one side.)

6. Do not aim the camera directly toward a light source.

7. Be sure that there is adequate light on the subject.

8. Remember to focus the camera carefully, concentrating on the main subject.

(Heinich, Molenda, Russell, and Smaldino, 1996, p. 94)

Extracurricular Event—"Education Week Displays"

Often, such as during an "Education Week," schools like to provide a means of showing to the community some educational events that are occurring within the schools. In response to a request from a local bank for displays of student work, various photography productions that had been completed during the year were set up in the bank lobby. Students were pleased to have their work displayed in such a visible place. Parents reported that they made several trips to view the displays themselves, and received many positive comments from friends and family regarding the obvious learning that had occurred during the production of the exhibits. The student and community response was positive and supportive!

References

Costa, A. 1985. Developing minds. In *Developing minds* (1985 Yearbook of the Association for Supervision and Curriculum Development) (chapter 4, pp. 46–58), edited by A. Costa. Washington, DC: ASCD.

Eisner, E. W. 1982. *Cognition and curriculum: A basis for deciding what to teach.* New York: Longman.

Hanson, J. R., H. F. Silver, and R. W. Strong. 1988. Learning styles and visual literacy: Connections and actions. In *Visual literacy in life and learning: Readings from the 19th Annual Conference of the International Visual Literacy Association* (pp. 270–98), edited by R. Braden, B. Braden, D. Beauchamp, and L. Miller. Blacksburg: Virginia Tech University.

Heinich, R., M. Molenda, J. D. Russell, and S. Smaldino. 1996. *Instructional media and technologies for learning.* Englewood Cliffs, NJ: Prentice-Hall.

Lacy, L. 1988. Thinking skills and visual literacy. In *Visual literacy in life and learning: Readings from the 19th Annual Conference of the International Visual Literacy Association* (pp. 33–40), edited by R. Braden, B. Braden, D. Beauchamp, and L. Miller. Blacksburg: Virginia Tech University.

Spoehr, K., and E. Lehmkuhle. 1982. *Visual information processing.* San Francisco: W. H. Freeman.

More Ideas

Curricular Areas **Production Ideas**

From *Technology Across the Curriculum.* © 1997. Marilyn J. Bazeli and James L. Heintz. Teacher Ideas Press. (800) 237-6124.

Activities

48 / Chapter 3: Photography/Transparency Activities

Pictorial Diaries

Objective
Students use photographs as a basis for a year-long personal diary or for a timeline of classroom events.

Overview
This activity can be done individually, as a personal record or diary of things important to the student during the school year. It can also be done as a group project, visually recording classroom events, which could then be placed on a timeline for display in the room. Students would be actively involved in selecting and producing appropriate visuals to represent events that occurred during the year.

Skill Areas
All Curricular Areas

Materials Checklist
- ☐ Camera (preferably automatic, for student use)
- ☐ Film

Adaptive Ideas
Students of all ages can engage in this activity. Younger children will need guidance with use of the camera. Older students should create more professional and interesting photographs, after additional instruction regarding composition of photos and visual elements of a "good" photograph.

Procedures
1. Begin with a discussion of "important events," what makes them important, and how to select events that can be visually recorded with a photograph. (If students are creating personal diaries, this discussion should be directed at those personal events that are milestones in the lives of the students. If students are working in groups to photograph classroom events, the discussion should be directed at the selection of events that are important to the classroom as a whole.)
2. Discuss guidelines for producing an effective photograph (see the introduction to this chapter). The depth of discussion should depend upon the maturity of the students. Discussion should center around the selection of a visual to represent in a photograph that clearly depicts the event that has been selected.
3. Students take photographs of selected events over time.
4. Students prepare either a pictorial diary or a classroom timeline using the photographs. For a diary, photos are mounted in an album or a student-made album using construction paper. For a classroom timeline, photos are mounted on poster board. Captions or descriptions can be added as necessary.
5. As new photographs are taken of continuing events during the year, those are added to the diary or timeline.

From *Technology Across the Curriculum.* © 1997. Marilyn J. Bazeli and James L. Heintz. Teacher Ideas Press. (800) 237-6124.

Evaluation

Select an appropriate evaluation form provided in appendix A. Projects can be evaluated in terms of selection of "important" events and the quality of the visual produced depicting that event. The evaluation standards should depend upon the maturity level of the students. (A rubric should be developed prior to production so that students know what the standards are.)

Teacher's Notes

Years activity implemented: _____

Discussion notes: _____

Comments for future use: _____

_____

_____

_____

_____

From *Technology Across the Curriculum.* © 1997. Marilyn J. Bazeli and James L. Heintz. Teacher Ideas Press. (800) 237-6124.

Visual Vocabulary

Objective
Students take photographs to visually define vocabulary words.

Overview
As new vocabulary words are introduced, in various curricular areas, students compose and produce a photograph of an object, place, or action that would visually define the word. For example, a vocabulary word *habitation* might be visually shown as a photo of a house or an animal home. The photos are stored in a classroom "visual dictionary."

Skill Areas
All Curricular Areas

Materials Checklist
- [ ] Camera
- [ ] Film
- [ ] Visual dictionary pages (construction paper, tagboard, etc.)
- [ ] Felt-tip markers

Adaptive Ideas
Older students might be challenged to find effective visual representations of the more abstract vocabulary words with which they will be dealing. Older students might also make individual visual dictionaries, rather than one for the class. Additionally, visuals might be displayed on bulletin boards before being put into a dictionary format.

Some curricular adaptations might include: English—defining parts of speech visually; math—defining geometric shapes as found in surroundings (for example, hexagon: floor tile); reading—defining specific vocabulary connected with a book or story.

Procedures
1. Students (individually or in a group) select or are assigned specific vocabulary words being presented in a given subject area.
2. Students identify some type of visual that would define their words.
3. Guidelines for effective photographs (as presented in the introduction to this chapter) are presented and discussed. Students take a picture of the identified visual to define their words.
4. Photographs are placed on a "dictionary" page, and students write (with marker) the vocabulary word next to the photo.
5. Pages are either assembled into one classroom dictionary, individual student dictionaries, or displayed on a bulletin board. These pages could be kept for many years, creating a large visual dictionary.

From *Technology Across the Curriculum.* © 1997. Marilyn J. Bazeli and James L. Heintz. Teacher Ideas Press. (800) 237-6124.

Evaluation

Select an appropriate evaluation form provided in appendix A. Completed photographs should be evaluated in terms of how well they define the given vocabulary word.

Teacher's Notes

Dates: _____

Subject: _____

Vocabulary words defined: _____

Comments for future use: _____

_____

_____

_____

_____

From *Technology Across the Curriculum.* © 1997. Marilyn J. Bazeli and James L. Heintz. Teacher Ideas Press. (800) 237-6124.

Making Science Visual

Objective
Students use photography to document specific aspects of science study.

Overview
Students select or are assigned a topic within the science area being studied. For example, if animals are being studied, sample topics might include: signs of animals, tracks of animals, animal homes, and so on. Students find and photograph examples of the topic.

Skill Areas
Science

Materials Checklist
- ☐ Camera
- ☐ Film
- ☐ Materials for mounting and labeling

Adaptive Ideas
All age levels can engage in this activity. The photographs might be used for display in the classroom as learning tools for other students. Photos might be used as part of extensive projects for portfolio or authentic assessment. Older students will be capable of producing professional-looking displays depicting more abstract topics.

The topic for a group of photos might be disclosed or left for viewers to discover (for example, seeing photos of beaver dams, birds' nests, beehives, and so on would lead viewers to conclude that the topic of the photos is "the homes of animals").

Procedures
1. Students are either assigned a topic or develop their own topic to represent visually (for younger students, the topic should be assigned).
2. Individually or in groups, students list ideas for visuals that might demonstrate their topic.
3. Students search out examples, using their lists as guides. Other examples, besides those listed, should also be found (the list provides a starting point).
4. Discuss guidelines for effective photographs (see the introduction to this chapter). Students take photographs of each of these visual examples.
5. Develop the photographs.
6. Students mount their photos on display boards, with brief descriptions. Or, students can provide no descriptions, involving viewers in the process of determining the topic represented.

From *Technology Across the Curriculum.* © 1997. Marilyn J. Bazeli and James L. Heintz. Teacher Ideas Press. (800) 237-6124.

Chapter 3: Photography/Transparency Activities / 53

Evaluation

Select an appropriate evaluation form provided in appendix A. Comprehension of the topic should be judged by the type of photos selected to represent the topic.

For Portfolios:

☐ Take photographs of the completed displays.

Teacher's Notes

Dates: _____

Topics: _____

Comments for future use: _____

_____

_____

_____

_____

_____

From *Technology Across the Curriculum.* © 1997. Marilyn J. Bazeli and James L. Heintz. Teacher Ideas Press. (800) 237-6124.

Visual Elements in Photos

Objective
Students use photography to document specific visual elements.

Overview
Students select or are assigned a topic—one specific element of a visual. Examples of such might include: color, shape, line, light, texture, pattern, shadow, perspective, framing, size, point of view and angle, or juxtaposition. Students find and photograph visuals depicting that element.

Skill Areas
Visual Literacy, Perception, Critical Viewing

Materials Checklist
- ☐ Camera
- ☐ Film
- ☐ Materials for mounting and labeling photographs

Adaptive Ideas
Students might be asked to find and photograph examples in designated places, such as within their own classroom, within the school and grounds, or anywhere in the community. All ages can participate.

Procedures
1. Students are either assigned or select a visual element to represent with photographs (younger students should be assigned an element, and it should be a concrete element such as shadow, color, or shape).
2. Individually or in groups, students search out examples of the visual element they will represent.
3. Students take photographs of these examples.
4. Have the photographs developed.
5. Students mount their photos on display boards, with a brief description of the visual element depicted. Or, students can provide no descriptions, involving viewers in the process of determining the topic represented.

From *Technology Across the Curriculum.* © 1997. Marilyn J. Bazeli and James L. Heintz. Teacher Ideas Press. (800) 237-6124.

Evaluation

Select an appropriate evaluation form provided in appendix A. Understanding of the visual element should be judged by the type of photos selected to represent that element.

For Portfolios:

☐ Take photographs of the completed displays.

Teacher's Notes

Dates: _____

Topics: _____

Comments/Ideas: _____

_____

_____

_____

_____

From *Technology Across the Curriculum*. © 1997. Marilyn J. Bazeli and James L. Heintz. Teacher Ideas Press. (800) 237-6124.

Mystery Enlargements

Objective
Students develop their visual perception and critical-viewing skills by photographing familiar objects at extremely close range and then sharing and discussing the photographs.

Overview
Students select objects in the classroom to photograph at close range. (Either photos or slides are appropriate; however, for effective class discussion, slides are better.) Classmates attempt to identify the object depicted in the photo or slide.

Skill Areas
Visual Literacy, Perception, Critical Thinking

Materials Checklist
- ☐ Camera (with macro lens or ability to focus close-up photos; see appendix C for equipment description)
- ☐ Film (slide film is recommended)

Adaptive Ideas
Younger students should be limited to objects in the classroom. Older students might select objects within the school or grounds or within the community.

Photographs or slides might be kept in a "visual perception library" for use with future classes.

Procedures
1. Select an object to be photographed. The selection process involves perception skills to determine what tiny object, or part of an object, would look different when greatly enlarged in a close-up photo.
2. Place the camera as close to the object or a segment of the object as the focusing capability will allow, and take the picture.
3. Students show their photos or slides to their classmates and ask them to identify the object.

From *Technology Across the Curriculum.* © 1997. Marilyn J. Bazeli and James L. Heintz. Teacher Ideas Press. (800) 237-6124.

Evaluation

Perception skills of students can be evaluated by observation. As this activity is repeated periodically, with all students having a chance to photograph objects close-up throughout the year, perception/acuity skills should show an increase.

Teacher's Notes

Dates: _____

Objects photographed: _____

Comments: _____

_____

_____

_____

_____

_____

From *Technology Across the Curriculum.* © 1997. Marilyn J. Bazeli and James L. Heintz. Teacher Ideas Press. (800) 237-6124.

History Through Photographs

Objective
Students produce a photographic record of specific events in history.

Overview
Individually or in groups, students select an event that occurred in connection with a particular historical time period being studied in class. Using a copystand and camera, photographs or slides are produced from pictures located in books, magazines, or other print materials. Selection of specific pictures relating to an event develops students' research skills. Selected photographs or slides are used in either a display or a presentation by the students.

Skill Areas
History, Group Cooperation, Research

Materials Checklist
- [ ] 35mm camera (with a macro lens)
- [ ] Film (print or slide film)
- [ ] Copystand (see appendix C for equipment description)
- [ ] Reference books, magazines, and other print media pertaining to the historical event

Adaptive Ideas
For younger children, a broad event, such as a particular president or space exploration, is more appropriate. For older children, a more specific event should be selected; examples might include: one battle of the Civil War, one scientific discovery in the life of a scientist, or one event in a president's term of office.

Procedures
1. Students select or are assigned an event to record with photographs.
2. Using research skills, students locate pictures pertaining to that event in as many reference materials as possible. Careful selection of pictures that specifically depict aspects of the event should be stressed. The purpose of using several types of reference materials is that students can pull together from different sources very specific visuals to aid in their display or presentation of the event.
3. Mount a 35mm camera with a macro lens on a copystand (see appendix C for equipment description). Using either print or slide film, students take pictures of the visuals found in the reference materials.
4. If print film was used, students either individually or in groups create a display with their finished photographs. The displays of specific events that are created by all of the students visually depict the entire historical time period being studied. If slide film was used, students use their finished slides for a presentation to the class about the specific event researched. All of the presentations combined provide students with visual as well as verbal information regarding a time period in history.

From *Technology Across the Curriculum.* © 1997. Marilyn J. Bazeli and James L. Heintz. Teacher Ideas Press. (800) 237-6124.

Evaluation

Select an appropriate evaluation form provided in appendix A. Displays and/or presentations should be evaluated in terms of how completely students researched the event and how precisely they selected photographs that accurately and specifically depict the event. Presentations skills might also be evaluated.

Teacher's Notes

Dates: _____

Time period studied: _____

Specific events researched: _____

Events difficult to research: _____

Events with many pictures available: _____

Events with few pictures available: _____

Notes regarding photographic displays: _____

Notes regarding slide presentations: _____

_____

_____

_____

_____

From *Technology Across the Curriculum.* © 1997. Marilyn J. Bazeli and James L. Heintz. Teacher Ideas Press. (800) 237-6124.

Visual Weather Records

Objective
Students record weather conditions over a specific time period with photographs.

Overview
Photography provides an ideal way to record changing weather. As students study the various ingredients that make up weather, some of these aspects can be recorded with photographs over a designated time period. Photographs should be taken in a specific place at a specific time each day for a month. Photographs might be taken of different cloud types as they occurred over six months, of different weather conditions as they occurred during a school year, and so on. As students are actively involved in visually recording changing weather conditions, they become more interested in studying the effect of these conditions on our planet.

Skill Areas
Science

Materials Checklist
- [ ] Camera
- [ ] Film
- [ ] Poster board
- [ ] Felt-tip markers
- [ ] Optional: Copystand (see Adaptive Ideas below; see appendix C for equipment description)

Adaptive Ideas
As briefly described in the Overview, this activity can be adapted in many ways. Additionally, it might be part of an ongoing observation of weather conditions, with dated charts containing instrument readings and pictures to record the weather over a time period. Also, students might focus on specific aspects of weather: interesting cloud formations, patterns of frost on a window, icicles, drifts in snow caused by wind patterns, sizes/shapes of rain puddles, runoff locations and patterns during/after a heavy rain, and so on.

If the teacher wants students to study a specific topic such as storms, and live examples of hurricanes or tornadoes cannot be photographed, a copystand could be used to photograph pictures in newspapers, magazines, and so on. (See appendix C for equipment description.)

Another adaptation of this activity, for older children, might be to study weather conditions in various locations. Newspapers or news magazines could be used to find pictures to be photographed using a copystand.

From *Technology Across the Curriculum.* © 1997. Marilyn J. Bazeli and James L. Heintz. Teacher Ideas Press. (800) 237-6124.

Procedures

1. Decide on the type of pictorial weather record to establish (recording weather conditions daily or weekly, concentrating on specific aspects such as clouds, frost, and so on).
2. Assign individual students or groups of students to be in charge of a specific time period to photograph or a particular aspect of weather to photograph.
3. Discuss guidelines for effective photographs (see the introduction to this chapter).
4. Develop the photographs. As photos are developed, assemble them onto poster boards, with dates, locations, labels for types of clouds, and other pertinent information.
5. Over time, students will be able to see weather changes with seasons and the effect of weather on our daily environment. When combined with instrument readings, students can see that a falling barometer one day may result in rain the next day, or that stratus clouds one day may result in rainy, nimbus clouds the next day.

Evaluation

Select an appropriate evaluation form provided in appendix A. Student work might be evaluated in terms of the accuracy and types of photographs chosen in fulfillment of the particular assignment. Accurate recording, labeling, and describing of pictures should also be a part of the evaluative process. Scientific record-keeping might be evaluated, especially for older children.

Teacher's Notes

Dates: _____

Time period recorded: _____

Specific aspects visually recorded: _____

Comments: _____

_____

_____

_____

_____

From *Technology Across the Curriculum*. © 1997. Marilyn J. Bazeli and James L. Heintz. Teacher Ideas Press. (800) 237-6124.

Rocks and Rock Formations

Objective
Students use photography to record various types of rocks and rock formations.

Overview
Many students have rock collections, and it is usually quite easy to have rocks on display in a classroom. However, very large rocks, sedimentary layers, and rock formations cannot be brought into the classroom. This activity encourages students to locate and record visually some natural formations or sedimentary layers. Students can discover those formations on their own or while on a field trip in a natural habitat.

Skill Areas
Science

Materials Checklist
- ☐ Camera (with a macro lens)
- ☐ Film
- ☐ Copystand (see appendix C for equipment description)
- ☐ Reference materials

Adaptive Ideas
Younger children might simply take pictures of interesting rocks or formations that they find. Older children might be assigned to take pictures of examples of specific types of rocks (such as sedimentary or metamorphic) or formations caused by water erosion, wind erosion, and so on.

Procedures
1. Organize the students into groups if a field trip will be conducted. If students will work on this on their own, in their own environment, they can work individually or in small groups.
2. Depending on the age of the students, either assign rocks and formations in general or assign specific types of rocks or formations to be photographed.
3. Students take their photographs.
4. Students find reference materials showing clear pictures of various types of rocks and formations.
5. Using a copystand with the camera and macro lens, students take photographs of the pictures found in reference materials.
6. Students create displays with their live and copystand photographs, depicting the particular rocks or formations assigned.

Evaluation

Select an appropriate evaluation form provided in appendix A. Students should be evaluated on their selection of photographs. Proper labeling and descriptions of rocks and formations should also be evaluated.

For Portfolios:

☐ Take photographs of the completed projects.

Teacher's Notes

Dates: _____

Field trip location: _____
or
Assignments/Specific rocks: _____

Comments/Ideas: _____

_____

_____

_____

_____

It's All in the Point of View

Objective

Students look at ideas or situations from varying points of view by creating pictures representing different points of view.

Overview

Students need to develop an awareness that there is more than one way to view a situation. This activity provides a visual way of involving students in this process. In this activity, students use photography to demonstrate various points of view. Such points of view could be: the playground from the point of view of a first-grader and the playground from the point of view of a teacher, or different points of view of characters in a book (one character seeing the neighborhood in terms of its interest and beauty, the other seeing it in terms of its poverty and hopelessness). Photographs are displayed and used as a basis for discussion.

Skill Areas

English, Literature, Critical Thinking, Visual Design

Materials Checklist

- ☐ Camera
- ☐ Film

Adaptive Ideas

This activity is best suited for older children because of the abstract thinking required. Students might create contrasting pictorial views of a character in a book versus a different character, views of a child contrasted to views of an adult regarding a particular issue, views of power (shown by a low-angle shot) and views of weak position (high-angle shot), and so on.

Simple concepts regarding point of view might be used with younger children; for example, they could show in photographs the point of view of an animal versus a human, a plant versus a human, or views from various locations within the classroom.

Procedures

1. An introductory activity to develop the concept of point of view might be necessary, depending upon the experience of the students. An activity that might prove effective is a discussion of the book *The True Story of the 3 Little Pigs by A. Wolf* as told to John Scieszka (New York: Viking Penguin, 1989).
2. A second introductory lesson should be to introduce students to different types of camera shots and uses of these shots, including:

    close-up: focuses on a single person or object

    long shot: depicts an entire area; shows location

high-angle shot: camera looks down on the subject; creates the illusion that the subject is small, inferior, or lonely

low-angle shot: camera is placed below the subject; creates the illusion that the subject is strong and superior

3. Students select or are assigned a focus for their pictorial point of view. Students could be asked to present only one point of view, with other students presenting an opposing point of view; or, students could present in one display contrasting points of view.

4. Students individually or in groups plan photographs that will demonstrate the point of view they are going to represent. Their planning should include the subjects to be photographed and the types of shots needed to show a particular point of view.

5. Take and develop the photographs.

6. The completed photographs are mounted on poster board for display in the classroom. If characters in a book have been used as the focus, the boards might also be displayed in the library.

7. Each completed display is discussed with other students regarding the concepts of point of view that are shown. The discussion can be led by the teacher or by the students who prepared the display.

Evaluation

Select an appropriate evaluation form provided in appendix A. Completed displays should be evaluated in terms of the types of visuals selected to represent a particular point of view. Both the subject of the visuals and the camera shot used in the photograph should be considered in the evaluation of the display.

Teacher's Notes

Dates: _____

Topics for point of view: _____

Comments/Ideas: _____

_____

_____

_____

_____

_____

From *Technology Across the Curriculum.* © 1997. Marilyn J. Bazeli and James L. Heintz. Teacher Ideas Press. (800) 237-6124.

Signs of the Seasons

Objective
Students develop a visual interpretation of changes or events during seasons of the year.

Overview
Seasons of the year involve both natural changes and events in connection with holidays. Students create a photographic representation of those changes and events. This activity helps students analyze, think critically, and appreciate these changes and events.

Skill Areas
Science, Visual Design, Social Studies

Materials Checklist
- ☐ Camera
- ☐ Film
- ☐ Poster board
- ☐ Reference materials

Adaptive Ideas
Students of all ages can engage in this activity. The types of visuals selected reflect the level of maturity of the students. Younger students should work with a broad concept, such as "winter"; older students should work with a more specific concept, such as "trees in winter" or "people in winter."

Procedures
1. Students select or are assigned a season of the year or a seasonal event (Thanksgiving, Christmas, etc.) to show in photographs. Within the selected topic, a specific focus might be added. For example, if Thanksgiving is the topic, a specific focus might be Food, Thankful Thoughts, or American Traditions. If Spring is the topic, a specific focus might be Spring Flowers, Signs of Spring, or Spring Weather. Other ideas might include: Winter Wonderland, New Year's Resolutions, Dreams for the Future, and Fall Changes.
2. Individually or in groups, students list things that might be photographed to depict their topic or focus within the topic.
3. Discuss guidelines for effective photographs (see the introduction to this chapter).
4. Students take their photographs.
5. Develop the photographs.
6. Photographs are mounted on poster board. The title of the topic may be given in the display or guessed by other students. Older students who selected a specific focus within a topic will benefit from discussion with classmates regarding how well they represented the chosen focus.

From *Technology Across the Curriculum.* © 1997. Marilyn J. Bazeli and James L. Heintz. Teacher Ideas Press. (800) 237-6124.

Evaluation

Select an appropriate evaluation form provided in appendix A. Critical thinking and analysis of the topic should be evaluated in terms of the visuals selected to depict that topic or focus within a topic.

Teacher's Notes

Dates: _____

Holiday: _____

    Specific focus: _____

Season: _____

    Specific focus: _____

Comments: _____

_____

_____

From *Technology Across the Curriculum.* © 1997. Marilyn J. Bazeli and James L. Heintz. Teacher Ideas Press. (800) 237-6124.

Let's Be Healthy!

Objective
Students create a visual chart demonstrating the importance of healthy foods, fitness, and exercise.

Overview
All aspects of health can be incorporated into this activity. Students create a photographic chart of foods within the food groups, correlate foods with particular organs of the body, show specific exercises, or display fitness activities.

Skill Areas
Health, Critical Thinking

Materials Checklist
- ☐ Health reference materials
- ☐ Camera (with macro lens)
- ☐ Copystand (see appendix C for equipment description)
- ☐ Film
- ☐ Poster board

Adaptive Ideas
Students of all ages can participate in some form of this activity. The teacher should adapt the activity depending upon the maturity of the students.

Procedures
1. Students select or are assigned a topic to show in photographs. Topics might include: foods and food groups, exercises, what parts of our body specific foods help, daily activities to stay fit, and so on.
2. Students, individually or in groups, discuss and list visuals they could use for photographs depicting their topic.
3. Using reference books and other materials, students locate pictures they can use to help visually represent their topic.
4. Using a copystand and camera with macro lens, students take photos of pictures or diagrams found in reference materials.
5. Students use the camera to take live photographs for use in the visual representation of their topic (see the introduction to this chapter for guidelines on effective photographs).
6. Have the photographs developed.
7. Photographs are mounted on poster board. Altogether, the displays, each showing a different topic related to health, form a complete visual reminder to students about the importance of health, proper foods, and exercise.

From *Technology Across the Curriculum.* © 1997. Marilyn J. Bazeli and James L. Heintz. Teacher Ideas Press. (800) 237-6124.

Evaluation

Select an appropriate evaluation form provided in appendix A. Health concepts should be evaluated by analyzing the visuals selected for display.

For Portfolios:

☐ Take photographs of the completed projects.

Teacher's Notes

Dates: _____

Health topics: _____

Comments: _____

_____

_____

_____

_____

_____

From *Technology Across the Curriculum.* © 1997. Marilyn J. Bazeli and James L. Heintz. Teacher Ideas Press. (800) 237-6124.

Slide Show of Our Community

Objective
Students take pictures of people or places within the school or community.

Overview
Students need to be aware of their surroundings, in their school and in their community. Many things make up these surroundings, such as buildings, people, organizations, and businesses. Students investigate and photograph various aspects of their community.

Skill Areas
Social Studies, Critical Thinking

Materials Checklist
- ☐ Camera
- ☐ Slide film
- ☐ Slide projector with carousel for slides

Adaptive Ideas
Younger children might focus on concrete elements of a community, such as businesses or buildings. Older children might focus on more specific or abstract elements, such as service organizations, occupations within the community, workers within a building, or special people within the community.

Procedures
1. Students select or are assigned a focus within the school or community.
2. Individually or in groups, students plan types of photographs that would demonstrate their particular focus.
3. Students (or the teacher) contact people to set up times for photographs, if necessary.
4. Discuss guidelines for effective photographs with the students (see the introduction to this chapter).
5. Take and develop the photographs as slides.
6. Students prepare a description to accompany their slides and practice oral presentation of the description.
7. Students present the slide show with live student descriptions to classmates or to other school/community groups.

From *Technology Across the Curriculum.* © 1997. Marilyn J. Bazeli and James L. Heintz. Teacher Ideas Press. (800) 237-6124.

Evaluation

Select an appropriate evaluation form provided in appendix A. Completeness of investigation into the particular focus of school or community should be evaluated, based on the photographs chosen to show that focus. The written description of the photographs and the oral delivery of the description might be evaluated for completeness, for writing skills, and for oral presentation skills.

Teacher's Notes

Dates: _____

Locations in the school/community: _____

People in the school/community: _____

Organizations in the school/community: _____

Businesses in the community: _____

Comments: _____

_____

_____

From *Technology Across the Curriculum.* © 1997. Marilyn J. Bazeli and James L. Heintz. Teacher Ideas Press. (800) 237-6124.

72 / Chapter 3: Photography/Transparency Activities

Effective Transparencies

Objective
Students learn to produce effective transparencies to enhance presentations in any curricular area.

Overview
Many people of all ages use transparencies in their presentations; however, often these transparencies are incorrectly produced and thus are ineffective as presentation tools. In this activity, students learn to correctly produce transparencies.

Skill Areas
All Curricular Areas

Materials Checklist
- ☐ Transparency film
- ☐ Markers
- ☐ Access to photocopy machine
- ☐ Optional: Computer (with text and graphic capability)

Adaptive Ideas
If a computer is available for student use, the transparencies can be designed using computer-generated text and graphics. From the print copy, a photocopy on transparency film can be made. If no computer is available, students can write text by hand, and use cut-and-paste techniques for graphic additions. A photocopy of their completed design can be made on transparency film.

Procedures
1. Present an introductory lesson on correct transparency production. Guidelines should include:
   - title at top
   - large print to be easily seen
   - picture or diagram for interest
   - horizontal format (eliminates top and bottom of screen)
   - only two or three main points
   - stress key words or ideas
   - do not use a lot of words
   - color can add interest or stress certain words

2. Students are each given an assignment to design (in connection with a particular topic being studied) a useful and effective transparency. Students handwrite or draw, use cut-and-paste methods, or use a computer to design a transparency on paper.

From *Technology Across the Curriculum.* © 1997. Marilyn J. Bazeli and James L. Heintz. Teacher Ideas Press. (800) 237-6124.

3. Make a transparency of each student's design. Students show their transparency to classmates for input and ideas.
4. Students complete their transparencies based on feedback and discussion from the class members.

Evaluation

Student-produced transparencies should be evaluated on the basis of how well they followed the guidelines set forth, how appropriate they were to the curricular area, and how correct they were in facts and spelling.

Teacher's Notes

Dates: _____

Topics presented: _____

Method of production: _____

Comments: _____

_____

_____

_____

_____

From *Technology Across the Curriculum.* © 1997. Marilyn J. Bazeli and James L. Heintz. Teacher Ideas Press. (800) 237-6124.

74 / Chapter 3: Photography/Transparency Activities

Projected Constellations

Objective
Students use an easy, projected visual to study constellations of stars.

Overview
Students use an overhead projector to visually represent a constellation of stars by punching holes in a sheet of paper. Light from the projector shines through the holes, thus projecting onto the screen an image of stars in a black sky. This is a quick and easy planetarium. Students present a report about the constellation.

Skill Areas
Science, English, Language Arts

Materials Checklist
- [ ] Paper
- [ ] Sharp objects for punching holes (nails of varying sizes, compasses, etc.)
- [ ] Overhead projector

Adaptive Ideas
As part of a creative writing project, students might design their own constellation, name it, and then write a detailed description, including where it is, when it can be seen, names of stars within the constellation, why the stars and constellation of stars are named as they are, and so on.

Procedures
1. Students research the topic of constellations, using books, magazines, NASA materials, and so on.
2. In groups or individually, students select or are assigned a specific constellation. Students write a report about that constellation, with information regarding location, where it can be observed in the sky at different times of the year, how it can be located, how it was named, any major stars within the constellation, distance from Earth, and so on.
3. Students sketch on a sheet of white paper the configuration of the constellation, with careful regard to the relative sizes of stars.
4. Using a sharp object, or several sharp objects if varying sizes of stars are required (objects such as different sizes of nails work well), students punch holes in the paper at the specific locations of the stars.
5. Place the paper on the overhead projector. Light passes through the holes, creating a clear image of a black nighttime sky, with the stars in the constellation illuminated.
6. Students present their report about the constellation while classmates view the constellation.

From *Technology Across the Curriculum.* © 1997. Marilyn J. Bazeli and James L. Heintz. Teacher Ideas Press. (800) 237-6124.

Evaluation

Select an appropriate evaluation form provided in appendix A. Reports should be evaluated for writing skills, for oral presentation skills, and for scientific content. The projected constellations should be evaluated in terms of their correctness, as part of the science study of constellations.

For Portfolios:

☐ Photocopy the written reports of each student.

Teacher's Notes

Dates: _____

Constellations presented: _____

Creative writing project dates: _____

Comments/Ideas for future use: _____

_____

_____

_____

_____

From *Technology Across the Curriculum.* © 1997. Marilyn J. Bazeli and James L. Heintz. Teacher Ideas Press. (800) 237-6124.

Professional-Quality Drawing with the Overhead Projector

Objective
Students create drawings to accompany reports by tracing a picture on the overhead projector.

Overview
Often, students want to include drawings with a report but lack the skill to create a drawing that clearly shows whatever the topic might be (animal, map, object, person, etc.). This activity allows the student to easily trace the outline of a picture and then use their own creativity to complete their drawing.

Skill Areas
All Curricular Areas

Materials Checklist
- ☐ Picture or diagram (single sheet or in a book)
- ☐ White paper
- ☐ Pencils
- ☐ Overhead projector

Adaptive Ideas
Students of all ages can use this technique for drawing. The quality of the finished product will depend upon the age of the students.

Procedures
1. The student selects a picture he or she wants to draw.
2. The student lays the picture on the stage of an overhead projector. Enough light from the projector shines through the picture that it can be seen by the student.
3. The student lays a piece of clear white paper (not construction paper, but a thinner paper, such as paper used for photocopying) over the picture.
4. With the light that shines through both sheets of paper, the student outlines the desired picture on the sheet of paper.
5. The student completes his or her drawing, using the original picture as a guide.

Evaluation

Selection of an appropriate picture to draw, for inclusion with a specific report, should be evaluated. A picture that clearly enhances the topic being investigated in the report would be considered a good choice.

Teacher's Notes

Dates: _____

Topics: _____

Location of original pictures: _____

Comments: _____

_____

_____

_____

_____

From *Technology Across the Curriculum.* © 1997. Marilyn J. Bazeli and James L. Heintz. Teacher Ideas Press. (800) 237-6124.

# Chapter 4
Audio Productions

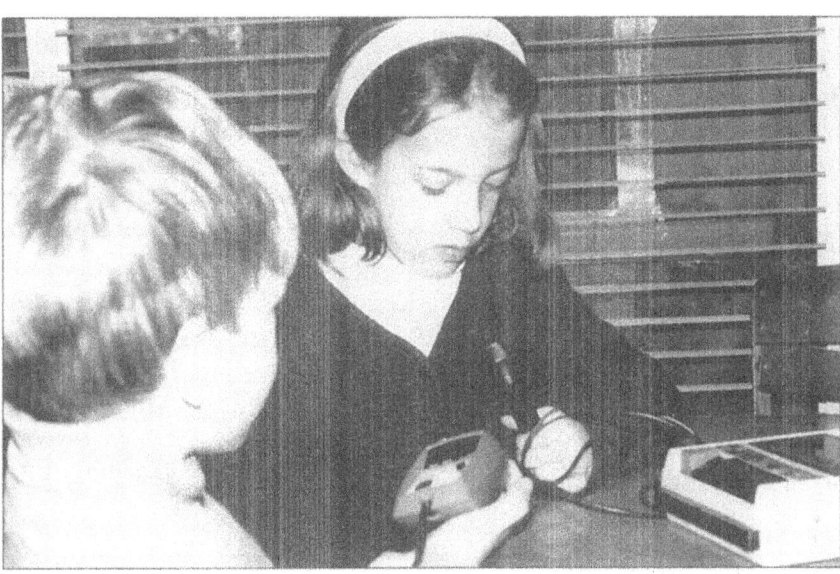

THE TAPE RECORDER HAS been in the classroom for many years. However, and unfortunately, the use of this technology has too often been limited to prerecorded presentations. Prerecorded presentations have made the tape recorder a very passive teaching tool. The activities presented in this chapter require the learner and the tape recorder to share an active role in the learning process.

Typically, elementary and secondary students presently spend about 50 percent of a school day just listening, while college students spend nearly 90 percent of their classroom time listening (Heinich, Molenda, Russell, and Smaldino, 1996). Therefore, it is important that critical analysis and production of audio media are not neglected.

Hearing and listening are not the same thing. Hearing involves the physical process of sound waves entering the ear and being transmitted to the brain. Listening is a psychological process, involving awareness of and attention to sounds, identifying and recognizing signals, and finally ending in comprehension.

Today, listening skills are being recognized as an extremely important part of learning. Just as critical viewing is necessary to be able to actively analyze the many visuals we receive daily, analyzing audio messages is also important. Active listening, for the purpose of critical thinking about what is heard, identifying and categorizing that message, and then comprehending and remembering the significant elements of the message are essential in today's world.

Because tape recorders are considered "old" technology, they are not often used in classrooms. However, the auditory recording of presentations can be an exciting motivator for students of all ages. The tape recorder can be very useful in any teacher's classroom because it is versatile, easy to use, and inexpensive.

The versatility of the tape recorder is an outstanding feature for use in the classroom. The tape recorder can be moved around the classroom very easily to accommodate individual, small-group, and entire-class use. Tape recorders are easy to store when not in use.

Yet another positive feature of the tape recorder is its cost. Tape recorders are an extremely inexpensive form of technology. All schools have tape recorders, most of which are probably not in use.

Before beginning any activities, some basic audio techniques should be presented and discussed with the students. See the sidebar "Basic Audio Production Skills."

In addition to the recording activities described in this chapter, listening skills should also be developed. As students listen to their peers' recordings, they can apply note-taking skills or memory skills to the activity. A lively discussion regarding the content of the audio cassette should be led by the teacher. In this way, students become active learners.

Extracurricular Activity— "Ask and Find Out"

One activity that always receives great evaluations is "Ask and Find Out." One fifth-grade class was extremely apprehensive about starting their next year at the middle school. There were many concerns about lockers, taking showers, passing to classes, and being in the hallways with older students. An arrangement was made with a sixth-grade English teacher at the middle school to exchange "Ask and Find Out" tapes. Fifth-grade students recorded questions about the upcoming school year in small groups. Six audio cassettes were sent to the middle school. The sixth-grade English class used the questions as a class assignment. The assignment required students to write and record answers to the fifth-grade students' questions. The English teacher related the fact that the real-life situations were a true motivator for her students. Likewise, the fifth-grade students were very satisfied with the answers they received as they dispelled many unwarranted fears.

References

Heinich, R., M. Molenda, J. D. Russell, and S. Smaldino. 1996. *Instructional media and technologies for learning*. Englewood Cliffs, NJ: Prentice-Hall.

Basic Audio Production Skills

1. Select an area for recording that is as free of noise as possible. A small room is better than a normal-size classroom because of fewer echoes. However, sound quality in a larger room could be helped by putting rugs or blankets on the floor, or hanging fabric over concrete walls in the recording area.

2. Be sure you are familiar with the specific tape recorder to be used. Practice using the controls before actually taping.

3. Record a short segment, rewind, and play back to check for volume and tone.

4. For best results, use a separate microphone, not one built into the tape recorder. Keep the microphone as far away from the recorder as possible. To protect against extraneous noises, place the microphone on a stand or soft cloth, and avoid handling the microphone. Speak *over* the microphone, not directly into it.

5. Keep the tape short—15 to 20 minutes at the longest, shorter for younger students.

6. Add appropriate sound effects, music, other voices, and so on, to add variety and realism (however, keep them to a minimum).

7. Speak with expression: Vary your tone of voice frequently, and speak cheerfully and enthusiastically.

8. Speak clearly, and avoid "uhs."

9. Practice what you want to say, but don't necessarily read it word-for-word unless you can do so with expression.

10. Record your presentation, then listen to it and critique your performance. Record again if necessary.

(Heinich, Molenda, Russell, and Smaldino, 1996, p. 188)

More Ideas

Curricular Areas   **Production Ideas**

Activities

Radio Review

Objective
Students create a radio program to review the facts of a unit of study in science, social studies, or health.

Overview
Students working in small groups prepare and record an audio cassette in an interview-style program to review a unit of study. The questions asked and answers given will demonstrate an understanding of the material studied.

Skill Areas
Oral Communication, Science, Social Studies, Health

Materials Checklist
- ☐ Tape recorder
- ☐ Audio cassette

Adaptive Ideas
Older students might be given questions in advance of a unit and prepare the interview as an assessment of their mastery of the unit.

Procedures
1. Small groups of students prepare questions and responses about a given topic.
2. Each group selects a person in the group to be the interviewer. The other students are a panel of experts on the topic and will answer the questions.
3. To add realism, the group prepares an introduction and a conclusion to the program, such as "It's Quiz Time."
4. Each group prepares answers to the questions. Answers should include many examples. (Groups demonstrating that they have gone beyond the objectives of the lessons by including outside research should be given extra credit.)
5. Record the presentations.
6. Play the tapes in class. The class evaluates the information to check for factual errors and to reinforce the learning of the material.

Evaluation

Select an appropriate evaluation form provided in appendix A.

Teacher's Notes

Dates: _____

Types of books used: _____

Remarks: _____

_____

_____

_____

_____

_____

From *Technology Across the Curriculum.* © 1997. Marilyn J. Bazeli and James L. Heintz. Teacher Ideas Press. (800) 237-6124.

86 / Chapter 4: Audio Productions

Ask and Find Out

Objective
Younger students write and record questions about topics older students are studying. Older students record answers and return them to the younger students.

Overview
Select a class at a younger level to ask questions of your class about a topic you are studying, such as dinosaurs, the Civil War, space exploration, and so on. The younger students record questions on audio cassette that your class will research and answer.

Skill Areas
Oral Communication, Research, Science, Social Studies, Health

Materials Checklist
- ☐ Tape recorder
- ☐ Audio cassette
- ☐ Research materials

Adaptive Ideas
The "Ask and Find Out" approach might be used with the principal, school librarian, senior citizens, parents, and so on asking the questions.

Procedures
1. Select a class at a younger level to ask questions of your class on a topic you are studying. The selected topic should be of high interest to the younger-level students.
2. Give the younger class an audio cassette to record questions to be researched by your class.
3. Once the tape is received, play it for your class. Students should select questions they would like to answer.
4. Older students research the answers to the questions. Answers should be written in language that is appropriate for the younger students.
5. Answers are recorded on a tape recorder. Older students might also prepare appropriate visual aids to accompany the answers.

From *Technology Across the Curriculum.* © 1997. Marilyn J. Bazeli and James L. Heintz. Teacher Ideas Press. (800) 237-6124.

Evaluation

Select an appropriate evaluation form provided in appendix A.

Teacher's Notes

Dates: _____

Types of units used: _____

Remarks: _____

_____

_____

_____

_____

_____

From *Technology Across the Curriculum.* © 1997. Marilyn J. Bazeli and James L. Heintz. Teacher Ideas Press. (800) 237-6124.

 # Math Jingles

Objective
Students write and record jingles about math facts.

Overview
Students create jingles about a set of math facts to aid in memorization. Students select a set of facts, such as the multiplication of 6s (6 x 1 = 6, 6 x 2 = 12, etc.). The idea is to create a jingle that will help all students remember the set. The jingles are recorded to assist others.

Skill Areas
Math, Creative Writing, Oral Communication

Materials Checklist
- ☐ Tape recorder
- ☐ Audio cassette

Adaptive Ideas
Older students might create jingles about spelling words or planets in the solar system.

Procedures
1. Divide the class into small groups and allow them to select a set of math facts they are having trouble memorizing.
2. Each group writes the facts so they have the correct problems and answers.
3. Each group writes a short jingle about all the facts or the ones that are the most difficult. Example: "Nine times nine is mighty fine, and eighty-one is the answer that is mine."
4. Each jingle is practiced and recorded on audio cassette to be shared with all students as a resource to aid in the memorization of a particular set of facts.

Evaluation

Select an appropriate evaluation form provided in appendix A.

For Portfolios:

☐ Photocopy the written jingle of each student.

Teacher's Notes

Dates: _____

Types of facts used: _____

Remarks: _____

_____

_____

_____

_____

_____

Public Service Announcement

Objective
Students research a community resource or health organization. Students write and record public service announcements to share the information.

Overview
Students research a community organization by contacting the organization directly or by research. Each group prepares and records a 30-second public service announcement to be played over the school's public address system. The public service announcement is used to create awareness of community resources.

Skill Areas
Oral Communication, Research, Community Awareness, Written Communication

Materials Checklist
- ☐ Tape recorder
- ☐ Audio cassette
- ☐ Access to the school's public address system
- ☐ Community service organization materials

Adaptive Ideas
Each group might create a bulletin board to accompany their public service announcement. At younger levels, students might prepare announcements about organizations that affect them, such as YMCA, community center, American Youth Soccer Organization, and so on.

Procedures
1. Divide students into small groups and decide on a community organization to research, such as Red Cross, Big Brothers/Big Sisters, Salvation Army, Homeless Shelters, and so on.
2. Each group contacts the organization directly to get the information that will be used in preparing the public service announcement.
3. Each group writes a 30-second public service announcement highlighting the organization's purpose, activities, and needs. The announcement should include how students can get involved in the organization if they are interested.
4. Record the announcements on audio cassette.
5. Play the announcements over the school's public address system.

Evaluation

Select an appropriate evaluation form provided in appendix A.

For Portfolios:

☐ Photocopy the written public service announcement of each student.

Teacher's Notes

Dates: _____

Types of organizations used: _____

Remarks: _____

_____

_____

_____

_____

_____

From *Technology Across the Curriculum.* © 1997. Marilyn J. Bazeli and James L. Heintz. Teacher Ideas Press. (800) 237-6124.

Radio News Update

Objective
Students prepare a radio news broadcast giving the current news, weather, and sports.

Overview
Students research, write, and present a radio news broadcast. Students record their broadcast on audio cassette.

Skill Areas
Written Communication, Oral Communication, Research, Reading

Materials Checklist
- ☐ Current newspapers or magazines
- ☐ Tape recorder
- ☐ Audio cassettes

Adaptive Ideas
Older students might present a research topic in a radio news broadcast format.

Procedures
1. Divide the class into small groups of three to five students.
2. Each group divides the news broadcast into categories to research, such as current news, weather, sports, community events, and commercials.
3. Each person in the group researches one of the categories for the broadcast.
4. Each person in the group writes a concise report for the category.
5. Each group practices the presentation of the broadcast as a team. Lively music, creative introductions, and broadcasting "radio" names (such as Records Renee, or Mad-dog Mike) can enhance the presentation.
6. Each group records the broadcast on audio cassette for later presentation or prepares a live-broadcast presentation from behind a screen to form a barrier from the audience. A microphone and speaker add realism to the presentation.

From *Technology Across the Curriculum.* © 1997. Marilyn J. Bazeli and James L. Heintz. Teacher Ideas Press. (800) 237-6124.

Evaluation

Select an appropriate evaluation form provided in appendix A.

For Portfolios:

☐ Photocopy the written report of each student.

Teacher's Notes

Dates: _____

Types of materials used: _____

Remarks: _____

_____

_____

_____

_____

_____

From *Technology Across the Curriculum.* © 1997. Marilyn J. Bazeli and James L. Heintz. Teacher Ideas Press. (800) 237-6124.

Halloween Sound Effect Stories

Objective
Students create a Halloween story complete with sound effects.

Overview
Halloween stories can be enhanced by sound effects, such as chains rattling, screams, and creaking doors. Students write and record scary Halloween stories with sound effects added to enhance the realism.

Skill Areas
Creative Writing, Communication Skills

Materials Checklist
- ☐ Tape recorder
- ☐ Audio cassette
- ☐ Sound effect materials (e.g., chains, objects to drop, and a squeaky hinge)

Adaptive Ideas
At lower grade levels, students might make sound effects while the teacher reads the story. The entire process could be recorded on audio cassette and played back for the students.

Procedures
1. Divide the class into small groups.
2. Each group writes a Halloween story. Each group should include sound effects in their stories.
3. Each group collects all the materials they will need to produce their sound effects.
4. Each group finds a quiet place to record their scary story.
5. Each group records their story on audio cassette, complete with sound effects at the appropriate places.
6. Play the tapes for the entire class in a darkened room.

From *Technology Across the Curriculum.* © 1997. Marilyn J. Bazeli and James L. Heintz. Teacher Ideas Press. (800) 237-6124.

Evaluation

Select an appropriate evaluation form provided in appendix A.

Teacher's Notes

Dates: _____

Types of books read: _____

Remarks: _____

_____

_____

_____

_____

_____

Speaker Stories

Objective
Students write creative stories or poems. The stories and poems are read using a microphone and a speaker for enhancement.

Overview
Students write stories or poems on a selected topic or on a topic of their own choice. Students read their stories and poems into a microphone that is attached to speaker/stereo system amplification and placed at the front of the classroom.

Skill Areas
Oral Communication, Creative Writing

Materials Checklist
- ☐ Microphone
- ☐ Stereo system (with microphone and speaker)

Adaptive Ideas
Students with musical talents might use a guitar or piano to accompany and enhance the story or poem.

Procedures
1. Assign a story/poem topic.
2. Set up a microphone and speaker at the front of the classroom to create a "performance" atmosphere.
3. Students practice reading into the microphone to test voice volume and proper positioning, as well as expression.
4. Students perform their stories and poems by reading them into the microphone. Tape record the performances of stories and poems on audio cassette.

Evaluation

Select an appropriate evaluation form provided in appendix A.

For Portfolios:

☐ Photocopy the story or poem of each student.

Teacher's Notes

Dates: _____

Types of stories created: _____

Remarks: _____

_____

_____

_____

_____

_____

From *Technology Across the Curriculum.* © 1997. Marilyn J. Bazeli and James L. Heintz. Teacher Ideas Press. (800) 237-6124.

"Good Morning" Announcements

Objective
Students demonstrate writing and speaking skills by preparing and presenting the school's morning announcements.

Overview
School announcements contain important information, but they can sometimes be unexciting. Students prepare school announcements that will attract attention. This activity might be done on a weekly basis or done for one week by one class and then by another class.

Skill Areas
Creative Writing, Interviewing Skills, Oral Communication

Materials Checklist
☐ Access to the school's public address system

Adaptive Ideas
Students might prepare announcements and record them on audio cassette to be played in classrooms.

Procedures
1. Create a system for students to collect information for the daily announcement (a box might be placed in the office or outside the classroom to collect potential announcements).
2. Students working in small groups rewrite the announcements in an interesting way that would appeal to most students' interest. The announcement might be created around a theme such as Halloween, a season, sports, and so on. Students create an introduction to the announcements to be used every day to call attention to the speaker.
3. All announcements are checked for accuracy before they are presented.
4. Each morning, students present the "Good Morning" announcements from the principal's office.

Evaluation

Select an appropriate evaluation form provided in appendix A.

For Portfolios:

☐ Photocopy the written morning announcement of each student.

Teacher's Notes

Dates: _____

Type of introductions used: _____

Remarks: _____

_____

_____

_____

_____

_____

From *Technology Across the Curriculum.* © 1997. Marilyn J. Bazeli and James L. Heintz. Teacher Ideas Press. (800) 237-6124.

One-Minute Reviews

Objective
Students record a one-minute review of a book they have read to create a file of reviews to encourage reading.

Overview
Each student records on audio cassette his or her review of a book that has just been read. The review should be one minute in length and should contain the student's impression of the book. The tapes will be cataloged to allow all students to hear reviews of books they would like to read. As other students read the book, they can add their review to the tape.

Skill Areas
Reading, Oral Communication, Written Communication

Materials Checklist
- ☐ Books
- ☐ Tape recorder
- ☐ Audio cassette

Adaptive Ideas
At high school levels, students might record book reports (reviews) on audio cassette for later evaluation.

Procedures
1. Assign students to read one of 10 books.
2. After students complete the book of their choice, they prepare a one-minute review of the book. Requirements for the review may be assigned as desired by the teacher.
3. Each student records the review on a tape labeled for the book that was read.
4. Additional reviews of the book are added to the tape as other students read the book.
5. Keep the tapes from year to year to encourage others to read the books on the list. Other students should listen to the reviews before reading the book themselves.

From *Technology Across the Curriculum.* © 1997. Marilyn J. Bazeli and James L. Heintz. Teacher Ideas Press. (800) 237-6124.

Evaluation

Select an appropriate evaluation form provided in appendix A.

Teacher's Notes

Dates: _____

Titles of the books used: _____

Remarks: _____

_____

_____

_____

_____

_____

From *Technology Across the Curriculum.* © 1997. Marilyn J. Bazeli and James L. Heintz. Teacher Ideas Press. (800) 237-6124.

Audio Pen Pals

Objective
Students correspond with pen pals by recording their "letters" on audio cassette.

Overview
This activity is an adaptation to writing letters to pen pals. Student send audio letters to their pen pals. Students write out the message in advance to provide clarity and organization to the letter. Tapes are exchanged and answered by their pen pals. NOTE: Students should already have pen pals that they exchange letters with on a regular basis.

Skill Areas
Oral Communication, Written Communication

Materials Checklist
- ☐ Tape recorder
- ☐ Audio cassette

Adaptive Ideas
Students might record letters for the principal or student council to answer and return.

Procedures
1. Provide each student a chance to write a short message for his or her pen pal that can be recorded on audio cassette. If possible, have one tape per student to allow for privacy.
2. Each student records his or her message on audio cassette. Each student should clearly identify who they are and whom they are sending the message to.
3. Tapes are exchanged and a response is recorded by the pen pal. Tapes can be exchanged back and forth on a regular basis, just as letters. Audio messages make a great addition to the pen-pal concept.

From *Technology Across the Curriculum.* © 1997. Marilyn J. Bazeli and James L. Heintz. Teacher Ideas Press. (800) 237-6124.

Evaluation

Select an appropriate evaluation form provided in appendix A.

Teacher's Notes

Dates: _____

Number of students per tape: _____

Remarks: _____

_____

_____

_____

_____

_____

From *Technology Across the Curriculum.* © 1997. Marilyn J. Bazeli and James L. Heintz. Teacher Ideas Press. (800) 237-6124.

Story Add-Ons

Objective
A small group of students begins a story on audio cassette. Other small groups of students add on to the story by recording more to the story. The process of adding on to the story continues until the story is completed.

Overview
A small group of students begins a story by recording it on audio cassette. The topic could be open or related to a current area of study. The tape is given to a second group to add on to the story. The process of adding on to the story continues from group to group until the story is ended.

Skill Areas
Oral Communication, Science, Social Studies, Health

Materials Checklist
☐ Tape recorder

Adaptive Ideas
Groups could create factual histories of events they research, such as Charles Lindbergh's preparation and flight over the Atlantic Ocean. Each group is responsible for one part of the event to add to the entire story.

Procedures
1. Divide the students into small groups.
2. Assign each group the beginning of a story. The story could be on a current topic of study or a creative fiction story.
3. Each group prepares the beginning of the story. The story should have definite characters and a well-defined setting. The story could be written out before taping or discussed among the group.
4. The beginning of the story is recorded on audio cassette. Each group should decide if the story is a narrative or if it will include dialogue.
5. Each group will exchange tapes with another group.
6. Each group listens to the beginning of the story as many times as necessary to understand the plot, characters, and setting.
7. Each group creates the next part of the story and records it on the audio cassette. The story should have continuity with the part previously recorded.
8. Repeat the process as many times as desired to complete the story.

From *Technology Across the Curriculum.* © 1997. Marilyn J. Bazeli and James L. Heintz. Teacher Ideas Press. (800) 237-6124.

Evaluation

Select an appropriate evaluation form provided in appendix A.

Teacher's Notes

Dates: _____

Types of stories used: _____

Remarks: _____

_____

_____

_____

_____

_____

From *Technology Across the Curriculum.* © 1997. Marilyn J. Bazeli and James L. Heintz. Teacher Ideas Press. (800) 237-6124.

Sixty-Second Great American

Objective
Students research the life of a great American and record a 60-second message stating why that person was or is a great American.

Overview
Students research a "Great American." The research needs to be condensed into a concise 60-second oral report stating the major accomplishment of the person. Reports are practiced, timed, and recorded.

Skill Areas
Oral Communication, Research, Written Communication, Social Studies, Science, Health

Materials Checklist
- ☐ Research materials
- ☐ Tape recorder
- ☐ Audio cassette
- ☐ Access to the school's public address system
- ☐ Optional: Stopwatch

Adaptive Ideas
The 60-second time limit might be expanded for younger children.

Procedures
1. Students work in small groups, pairs, or individually.
2. Students select a "Great American" to research. Topics could include presidents, inventors, heroes, or scientists.
3. Students condense the information they find on the "Great American" into a 60-second report. The material selected should state why the person is a "Great American."
4. Students practice their report orally to check for the required time limit. Using a stopwatch is a great motivator.
5. Students record the "Great American" report on audio cassette to be played for the entire class.
6. Play the reports one per day over the school's public address system to create awareness of the individuals.

From *Technology Across the Curriculum*. © 1997. Marilyn J. Bazeli and James L. Heintz. Teacher Ideas Press. (800) 237-6124.

Evaluation

Select an appropriate evaluation form provided in appendix A.

For Portfolios:

☐ Photocopy the "Great American" written report of each student.

Teacher's Notes

Dates: _____

Types of "Great Americans" selected: _____

Remarks: _____

_____

_____

_____

_____

_____

From *Technology Across the Curriculum.* © 1997. Marilyn J. Bazeli and James L. Heintz. Teacher Ideas Press. (800) 237-6124.

News Flash

Objective
Students record an important fact or facts on a given day.

Overview
Groups of students research important events for each day of the month. Students' personal information, such as birthdays, is included. Each group records one month on an audio cassette. Each day, the tape is played, giving the fact or facts of the day.

Skill Areas
Research, Oral Communication, Written Communication

Materials Checklist
- ☐ Tape recorder
- ☐ Audio cassette
- ☐ Research materials (encyclopedias, etc.)
- ☐ Calendars

Adaptive Ideas
A topic area might be selected for the focus of the facts, such as scientists, political leaders, inventions, and so on. Students record significant facts that happened during one month.

Procedures
1. Divide the class into small groups of two or three students.
2. Assign each group of students one month of the year to research.
3. Each group begins with a list of the days of the months.
4. Birthdays of the class are written first. Likewise, any other significant class information that could be included should be given to the proper group.
5. Each group researches encyclopedias, calendars, and other reference materials to find events to record for each day of the month.
6. Record the month's information on audio cassette, such as "March 12th—It's John's birthday and the Girl Scouts were founded on this date."
7. Each day, play the portion of the tape for the given date. The facts could be used as discussion topics and writing ideas.

Evaluation

Select an appropriate evaluation form provided in appendix A.

Teacher's Notes

Dates: _____

Types of reference materials used: _____

Remarks: _____

_____

_____

_____

_____

_____

From *Technology Across the Curriculum.* © 1997. Marilyn J. Bazeli and James L. Heintz. Teacher Ideas Press. (800) 237-6124.

110 / Chapter 4: Audio Productions

Personal Journal

Objective
Each student keeps an audio journal of the current school year.

Overview
Each student will have his or her own audio cassette. Students record messages to themselves about events of the school year. Each entry is dated. Information can include recording of writings, poems, grades on tests, reactions to projects worked on, activities played in gym, songs sung in music, and so on.

Skill Areas
Oral Communication

Materials Checklist
☐ Tape recorder
☐ Audio cassettes

Adaptive Ideas
Parent volunteers, teacher aides, or older students might assist younger students in taping an appropriate message.

Procedures
1. Label one audio cassette for each student with name, grade, year of school, and teacher's name. All tapes are stored in a convenient place to allow students easy access.
2. Rules are established regarding the use of the tapes, such as using only their own tape, never to rewind the tapes, and when they may be used.
3. Each student retrieves his or her own tape at any time of the day and records a special message about the happenings of the day. Information can include recording of writings, poems, grades on tests, reactions to projects worked on, activities played in gym, songs sung in music, and so on. Students include the current date for each recording.
4. Tapes can be taken home at the end of the year as an audio diary of their school year.

From *Technology Across the Curriculum.* © 1997. Marilyn J. Bazeli and James L. Heintz. Teacher Ideas Press. (800) 237-6124.

Evaluation

Students should write a note regarding any problems with the projects. Also ask for parent responses at the end of the year.

Teacher's Notes

Dates: _____

Remarks: _____

_____

_____

_____

_____

_____

_____

From *Technology Across the Curriculum.* © 1997. Marilyn J. Bazeli and James L. Heintz. Teacher Ideas Press. (800) 237-6124.

Guess the State

Objective

Students research, write, and record 10 facts about one of the 50 states. Tapes are played and the class can attempt to guess the name of the state.

Overview

This is an activity to share with other classes, and to motivate students to research one of the 50 states. Small groups of students should research 10 facts about the state. Facts should include major crops, resources, landmarks, cities, and so on. The 10 facts are recorded on audio cassette. The tapes are exchanged with other classes studying the states. The tapes are played and the class tries to guess the state.

Skill Areas

Social Studies, Research, Writing, Oral Communication

Materials Checklist

- [ ] Tape recorder
- [ ] Audio cassette
- [ ] Encyclopedias and state reference materials

Adaptive Ideas

The same procedure might be used for countries, famous people, animals, dinosaurs, and so on.

Procedures

1. Select two classes to play "Guess the State."
2. Divide each class into small groups and give each a state to research.
3. Each group researches 10 facts that describe the state. The clues should describe the state's natural resources, major crops, products produced, major landforms, interesting landmarks, and major cities.
4. Each group records the 10 facts on audio cassette. The number should be stated at the beginning of the recording, such as "State number 1, can you guess this state?"
5. Clues are ordered by difficulty, with the hardest clues given first.
6. Create an answer key.
7. Tapes and the answer key are exchanged and the game is played in each classroom.

From *Technology Across the Curriculum.* © 1997. Marilyn J. Bazeli and James L. Heintz. Teacher Ideas Press. (800) 237-6124.

Evaluation
Each class should make comments about the difficulty in finding the answer to the clues.

Teacher's Notes

Dates: _____

Types of books read: _____

Remarks: _____

_____

_____

_____

_____

_____

From *Technology Across the Curriculum.* © 1997. Marilyn J. Bazeli and James L. Heintz. Teacher Ideas Press. (800) 237-6124.

Chapter 5
Computer Activities

THE COMPUTER REVOLUTION is definitely upon all aspects of society, including education. The number of computers in the schools steadily increases each year. Education futurists, such as Lewis Perelman (1992), state that the rapid growth of information technology will force restructuring of the way we do things in school. Many schools are already involved in setting up problem-oriented environments, with students working cooperatively to solve computer-simulated problems. The possibility that students in school today will need to be able to operate computers in their post–high school job in some capacity is almost a certainty. Therefore, teaching effective and creative uses of the computer is imperative for teachers.

As teachers prepare students to be productive, active members of society, the need for a knowledge of computers and computer capability is essential. Students need to learn computer skills that demonstrate they are in control of the functions of the computer. Students should view the computer as a tool or source of information they, themselves, control. Unfortunately drill-and-practice software still dominates the uses of computers in most schools. The learner is guided by the software and responds when prompted.

Seymour Papert (1980), the originator of the LOGO procedural language for computers, stated that a computer should be an object to think with rather than a dispenser of information. Using LOGO, students can develop a sense of mastery over the computer and their environment, which promotes understanding. Today, many school reform advocates believe that use of the computer can develop critical-thinking and problem-solving skills in students, if the computer is properly used in learning activities. They also believe that students need to be able to access, manipulate, organize, and evaluate information. "Students should be prepared to be active life-long learners, engaging in authentic tasks and producing realistic projects" (Heinich, Molenda, Russell, and Smaldino, 1996, p. 234).

The activities presented in this chapter use the computer as a learning tool. The computer and software uses are a means to communicate, learn, and think. The activities also demonstrate that children can use the computer in small-group settings. Likewise, the activities show that the computer should be integrated into the learning environment—the classroom. The computer needs to be as available for the students as books, dictionaries, reference materials, and teachers.

115

Computers are a definite part of everyday life. The cost of computer equipment and software continues to decrease, allowing more and more schools to add more and more equipment. However, the impact of computers on education will depend on the extent to which they are used as learning tools. The effective use of computers in education will come from the student recognizing, through well-designed activities, that the computer is a tool he or she can manipulate to accomplish a goal.

Teachers no longer need to assume the role of information-giver, but rather need to be the guides and facilitators of learning. Computers, if properly used, can provide students and teachers with a tool to help create schools as places to learn *how* to learn.

Extracurricular Activity— "How to Spend a Million Dollars"

"How to Spend a Million Dollars" was a great way to introduce the power of a spreadsheet. (See fig. 5.1.) Math groups were assigned the task of spending *exactly* one million dollars, given a specific set of items. First, groups worked using the pencil-and-paper method. Each group recorded a few trials at spending the million dollars, but made errors in keeping track of all the steps. The second activity involved the use of calculators. The number of trials increased, estimating was used more effectively, and less frustration was exhibited. The final activity used a simple spreadsheet that multiplied the number of items times the amount of the item. The spreadsheet also summarized the total. Each group was able to see the benefits of estimation more clearly. All groups were within dollars of the total in just a few minutes. Several groups solved the exercise. Some advanced students asked about the structure of the spreadsheet. After a short explanation, they were using the spreadsheet to multiply, add, subtract, and total. Many students applied their learning of the "million dollar" activity to other situations. This application to other learning situations demonstrates that they had integrated the spreadsheet technique into their problem-solving skills and critical-thinking approaches. Students evaluated the entire project with high marks. The answer is given below.

References

Heinich, R., M. Molenda, J. D. Russell, S. Smaldino. 1996. *Instructional media and technologies for learning.* Englewood Cliffs, NJ: Prentice-Hall.

Papert, S. 1980. *Mindstorms: Children, computers, and powerful ideas.* New York: Basic Books.

Perelman, L. J. 1992. *School's out: A radical new formula for the revitalization of America's educational system.* New York: Avon.

How to Spend a Million Dollars: Answer

Island: 1; Yacht: 1; Car: 4; Motorcycle: 23; CD Player: 75; Bicycle: 90; Video Game: 76; Movie: 26; Sports Cards: 40.

How to Spend a Million Dollars

Spend exactly one million dollars without going over that amount. You must buy at least one of each item.

Item	Quantity	Cost/Item	Total
Island	_____	$656,654.67	_____
Yacht	_____	$214,076.88	_____
Car	_____	$17,004.91	_____
Motorcycle	_____	$1,406.25	_____
CD Player	_____	$179.58	_____
Bicycle	_____	$124.06	_____
Video Game	_____	$49.95	_____
Movie	_____	$14.96	_____
Sport Cards	_____	$2.15	_____

Total _____

Method Used: _____
_____
_____

Student Observations: _____
_____
_____

Teacher Observations: _____
_____
_____
_____

Fig. 5.1. How to Spend a Million Dollars worksheet.

From *Technology Across the Curriculum.* © 1997. Marilyn J. Bazeli and James L. Heintz. Teacher Ideas Press. (800) 237-6124.

More Ideas

Curricular Areas   **Production Ideas**

Activities

Draw Me a Story Starter

Objective
Each student creates an original picture on a drawing program. Students write creative stories to accompany their pictures.

Overview
Students love to create original pictures using simple drawing software. Most drawing software includes graphics that can be placed within the drawing to aid in the completion of pictures. The pictures will be printed out (in color if possible). Each student writes a creative story to accompany the picture. Both the picture and story are displayed.

Skill Areas
Drawing, Creative Writing

Materials Checklist
- ☐ Computer drawing software
- ☐ Word-processing software
- ☐ Printer

Adaptive Ideas
For younger students, have parent volunteers or older students (computer tutors) assist in the drawing of the picture.

Procedures
1. Divide the class into student pairs or allow students to work on an individual basis to create a picture using drawing software.
2. Print out the pictures that are created. Students should color the pictures if a color printer is not available.
3. Students use the pictures as story starters for a creative writing assignment.
4. Students write their stories using word-processing software (use paper and pencils if word-processing software is not available).
5. Display the stories with the pictures.

From *Technology Across the Curriculum.* © 1997. Marilyn J. Bazeli and James L. Heintz. Teacher Ideas Press. (800) 237-6124.

Evaluation

Select an appropriate evaluation form provided in appendix A.

For Portfolios:

☐ Make a copy of the story and picture created by each student.

Teacher's Notes

Dates: _____

Types of books used: _____

Remarks: _____

_____

_____

_____

_____

_____

From *Technology Across the Curriculum.* © 1997. Marilyn J. Bazeli and James L. Heintz. Teacher Ideas Press. (800) 237-6124.

122 / Chapter 5: Computer Activities

Electronic Notes

Objective
Students use word-processing software to record information learned while exploring topics. The information is printed for all members of the group and class.

Overview
Small groups or investigative teams of students research a topic in science or social studies. Each group or team records all information found, as well as notes given in class. The entire file is edited to create a concise report on the topic.

Skill Areas
Science, Social Studies, Health, Organization, Word Processing

Materials Checklist
- ☐ Word-processing software
- ☐ Printer
- ☐ Research materials

Adaptive Ideas
Notes given in class lectures might be recorded in a word-processing file for students who are absent or for those students who have difficulty taking or organizing notes.

Procedures
1. Divide the class into investigative teams at the beginning of a new topic or area of study.
2. Each team records notes given by the teacher into a word-processing file. The group adds to the file information taken from research materials, textbooks, experiments and simulations, movies and videos, and so on.
3. Each team adds "extras"—information found that goes beyond the objectives of the unit. On an ongoing basis, each team should edit and reorganize the notes.
4. Print out the notes at the end of the unit, to be studied or included in a portfolio of information.

From *Technology Across the Curriculum.* © 1997. Marilyn J. Bazeli and James L. Heintz. Teacher Ideas Press. (800) 237-6124.

Evaluation

Select an appropriate evaluation form provided in appendix A.

Teacher's Notes

Dates: _____

Types of subjects researched: _____

Remarks: _____

_____

_____

_____

_____

_____

From *Technology Across the Curriculum.* © 1997. Marilyn J. Bazeli and James L. Heintz. Teacher Ideas Press. (800) 237-6124.

Computer Tutors

Objective
Students become software tutors for students in lower grades.

Overview
Many teachers would like their students to work on various pieces of software. However, the teachers feel they do not know the operation of all the different types of software. This activity would allow older students to learn different software programs and become "experts" and a resource for teachers with young students. The "expert" student would be available to assist younger students in learning how to operate new pieces of software.

Skill Areas
Oral Communication, Computer Skills

Materials Checklist
☐ Various computer software programs

Adaptive Ideas
"Expert" students might become assistants in the learning center or other areas that have computers.

Procedures
1. Select a class to offer your students services as "Computer Tutors." This situation needs to be mutually agreed upon by both teachers.
2. Students, working in small groups, should train on software that younger students will be using.
3. Students must demonstrate proficiency on all pieces of software available to the younger students. A proficiency card and certificate should be given to the students who demonstrate they are "experts."
4. Students and teachers schedule times to work with the younger class.
5. Students keep a log of the software worked on and the type of training that was given on each visit.

Evalation
Select an appropriate evaluation form provided in appendix A.

Teacher's Notes

Dates: _____

Classes/Teachers used: _____

Remarks: _____

_____

_____

_____

_____

_____

From *Technology Across the Curriculum.* © 1997. Marilyn J. Bazeli and James L. Heintz. Teacher Ideas Press. (800) 237-6124.

Who's Read That?

Objective
Students use database software to record all the books that they read.

Overview
Students record the books that they read into a database. Students also record the type of book, main character, and their own reactions. Database-sorted lists can be prepared to show the books that have been read and to stimulate interest in reading.

Skill Areas
Reading, Evaluating, Database Management

Materials Checklist
- ☐ Database software
- ☐ Printer
- ☐ Books

Adaptive Ideas
Younger students will need volunteer parents, teachers, or older students (computer tutors) to enter the author, title, type of book, and a student rating on the book into the database. Lists can be prepared to encourage all students to read and to track each of the books that have been read.

Procedures
1. Develop a book rating system with the entire class. The system should be simple, such as 1–5, with 5 indicating "excellent" and 1 indicating "poor."
2. Develop a database that includes categories such as title, author, type of book, rating score, and other categories that fit the individual class.
3. Students track the books they read by recording the author, title, type of book, and rating score into a database file.
4. Book lists are printed on a weekly or monthly basis to encourage others to read the same books. Lists can easily be generated by author, title, type of book, or rating score.

From *Technology Across the Curriculum*. © 1997. Marilyn J. Bazeli and James L. Heintz. Teacher Ideas Press. (800) 237-6124.

Evaluation

Select an appropriate evaluation form provided in appendix A.

Teacher's Notes

Dates: _____

Types of books read: _____

Remarks: _____

_____

_____

_____

_____

_____

From *Technology Across the Curriculum.* © 1997. Marilyn J. Bazeli and James L. Heintz. Teacher Ideas Press. (800) 237-6124.

128 / Chapter 5: Computer Activities

How to Spend a Million Dollars

Objective
Students use spreadsheet software to calculate how to spend exactly one million dollars.

Overview
Students are given eight items to buy in any quantities desired. The objective is to spend *exactly* one million dollars, or as close to one million dollars as possible without going over. Those coming closest to one million dollars are the winners. The purpose is to see the power of recalculation using spreadsheet software.

Skill Areas
Math, Estimating

Materials Checklist
- ☐ Worksheets (Fig. 5.1 on page 117)
- ☐ Spreadsheet software
- ☐ Calculators

Adaptive Ideas
Students might calculate the price of items with shipping and handling and taxes.

Procedures
1. Give students a copy of a worksheet (fig. 5.1). Allow students one day to find exactly one million dollars in expenses. There is only one rule: They must have at least one of each item. Have students use the paper-and-pencil method first.
2. Have students repeat the exercise using a calculator to aid in solving the problem.
3. Set up a simple spreadsheet that multiplies items needed by cost per item and then sums the total. Also, create a spreadsheet cell that subtracts the grand total from $1,000,000 to show the current amount over or under.
4. Students record the number of trials using each method.
5. Students record their observations and compare the three methods used to solve the problem.

From *Technology Across the Curriculum*. © 1997. Marilyn J. Bazeli and James L. Heintz. Teacher Ideas Press. (800) 237-6124.

Evaluation

Evaluate the student's observations and comparisons of the methods.

For Portfolios:

☐ Photocopy the activity sheet of each student.

Teacher's Notes

Date: _____

Type of software used: _____

Remarks: _____

_____

_____

_____

_____

_____

From *Technology Across the Curriculum.* © 1997. Marilyn J. Bazeli and James L. Heintz. Teacher Ideas Press. (800) 237-6124.

Goal of the Week

Objective
Students use word-processing software for goal setting and recording observations on their progress.

Overview
Students set goals for the week through committees or group discussions. The goal of the week should be something the class wants to achieve. The goal is entered into a word processor and dated. At the end of the week, students record their observations on the progress that was made toward accomplishing the goal.

Skill Areas
Group Discussion, Goal Setting, Word Processing

Materials Checklist
- ☐ Word-processing software
- ☐ Printer

Adaptive Ideas
Older students might set individual goals. Students involved in extracurricular programs might want to set goals in these areas as well.

Procedures
1. Set up small committees of students to discuss setting a goal for the classroom for the week.
2. Each week, select a goal for the class to achieve and discuss what needs to be accomplished.
3. The committees enter the goal of the week into the word-processing file and print copies to be displayed on a bulletin board.
4. At the end of the week, the class discusses the progress made toward successfully accomplishing the goal of the week.
5. Students' reactions to the success of the goal of the week are entered into the word-processing file and printed. The printout is displayed for further review. A logbook containing each goal and student reactions should be kept throughout the year.

Evaluation

The logbook should be reviewed by parents, other teachers, administrators, and students. Additional reactions and feedback should be given to the class by anyone who reads the logbook. Teachers use reflective assessment techniques in their review of progress of the students.

Teacher's Notes

Dates: _____

Type of goal selected: _____

Remarks: _____

_____

_____

_____

_____

_____

From *Technology Across the Curriculum.* © 1997. Marilyn J. Bazeli and James L. Heintz. Teacher Ideas Press. (800) 237-6124.

What's My Grade?

Objective
Students use simple spreadsheet software to monitor their scores and averages of test grades in a particular subject.

Overview
Students construct a simple spreadsheet to keep track of the test grades in a particular subject, such as math or spelling. Students estimate changes in their overall average by entering possible grades on future tests and observing the changes in the average. This activity gives practice in interpreting statistical information.

Skill Areas
Math, Estimating, Averaging

Materials Checklist
☐ Spreadsheet software

Adaptive Ideas
Print out the test information, including averages. Students might prepare graphs to represent their testing scores and changes in average.

Procedures
1. Construct a simple spreadsheet that adds a column of numbers and finds a simple average. Older students should create their own spreadsheets.
2. Create a file for each student in the class.
3. Each student should enter his or her test scores into the spreadsheet as they are received to keep track of his or her average.
4. Students make predictions in the change of their average by substituting possible scores in the future test-result cells. Students should experiment with entering 100 into the next text cell to see the effect of a perfect score. The experiment should be repeated for receiving scores such as 90, 80, 70, and so on.
5. Students write the possible changes in their test average in paragraph form.

From *Technology Across the Curriculum.* © 1997. Marilyn J. Bazeli and James L. Heintz. Teacher Ideas Press. (800) 237-6124.

Evaluation

Select an appropriate evaluation form provided in appendix A.

Teacher's Notes

Dates: _____

Type of software used: _____

Remarks: _____

_____

_____

_____

_____

_____

From *Technology Across the Curriculum.* © 1997. Marilyn J. Bazeli and James L. Heintz. Teacher Ideas Press. (800) 237-6124.

134 / Chapter 5: Computer Activities

Getting to Know You

Objective
Students search information entered into a database as a way to get to know each other.

Overview
Information about each individual in the class is entered into a database. Searches are made to determine students with similar interests.

Skill Areas
Logic, Self-Awareness, Group Awareness, Database Management

Materials Checklist
- ☐ Database software
- ☐ Printer
- ☐ Questionnaire (see "Procedures")

Adaptive Ideas
Older students might survey the entire grade level as to possible interests in clubs, organizations, and sports. Lists might be formulated to get students involved in their school community.

Procedures
1. Students in the class generate a list of personal characteristics for a questionnaire. Example characteristics might include number of brothers, number of sisters, favorite foods, favorite sports, types of books read, and so on. List at least 20 characteristics on the questionnaire.
2. The questionnaire is duplicated for all members of the class, the teacher, parent volunteers, and so on.
3. Students enter the information from the questionnaires into the database (some students, if skill level and time permit, might enter the information directly into the database).
4. Students generate lists of characteristics to find the common interests of the class to promote group awareness. Searches can be done in more than one category, such as those who like pizza *and* root beer, or those who have a cat *and* like to read.

From *Technology Across the Curriculum*. © 1997. Marilyn J. Bazeli and James L. Heintz. Teacher Ideas Press. (800) 237-6124.

Evaluation

Select an appropriate evaluation form provided in appendix A. Lists might be shared with parents at the beginning of the school year and again later in the year. Student changes or progress, over time, might be assessed.

Teacher's Notes

Dates: _____

Personal characteristics assessed: _____

Remarks: _____

_____

_____

_____

_____

_____

From *Technology Across the Curriculum.* © 1997. Marilyn J. Bazeli and James L. Heintz. Teacher Ideas Press. (800) 237-6124.

Open House/Conference Notes

Objective
Students create a series of screens using presentation software, to be played at "Open House," assemblies, or parent-teacher conferences.

Overview
Small groups of students create screens of information that all parents need to know. The screens are linked together to prepare an organized presentation of information. The presentation is made available for all parents to view during "Open House," assemblies, or parent-teacher conferences.

Skill Areas
Organization, Written Communication, Drawing

Materials Checklist
☐ Presentation software

Adaptive Ideas
High school students might create presentations for elementary school teachers. Students should gather the information that the elementary school teacher wants to be displayed.

Procedures
1. Hold a group meeting to discuss the information that all parents should be given at "Open House," assemblies, or parent-teacher conferences. Examples might be "Check for needed school supplies," "Remember the School Fun Fair," "The class needs old newspapers for a project in November," or "Study the weekly spelling words."
2. Assign each area of information to a small group of students.
3. Each group designs a presentation screen to communicate the necessary information.
4. Groups link the completed presentation screens together to form a complete presentation.
5. One student from each group is elected to operate the program or to write specific instructions for parents.

From *Technology Across the Curriculum.* © 1997. Marilyn J. Bazeli and James L. Heintz. Teacher Ideas Press. (800) 237-6124.

Evaluation

Select an appropriate evaluation form provided in appendix A.

Teacher's Notes

Dates: _____

Type of software used: _____

Remarks: _____

_____

_____

_____

_____

_____

From *Technology Across the Curriculum.* © 1997. Marilyn J. Bazeli and James L. Heintz. Teacher Ideas Press. (800) 237-6124.

Computer Pen Pals

Objective
Students correspond with pen pals using word-processing software.

Overview
This activity mixes word-processing skills with letter-writing practice. Students write letters to their pen pals using word-processing software. The files are saved to diskette and sent to the pen pals. The files are answered by the pen pals and then returned to students. (NOTE: Students must currently have pen pals that they write to on a regular basis.)

Skill Areas
Word Processing, Written Communication, Proofreading

Materials Checklist
☐ Word-processing software

☐ Diskettes (one for each student)

Adaptive Ideas
Students might use on-line services or E-mail to send letters to their pen pals.

Procedures
1. Provide each student with a diskette.
2. Students practice their word-processing skills, such as centering, underlining, spell-checking, and so on, as they enter their letters to their pen pals.
3. Students proofread their letters. Peer editing is acceptable, depending on the content of the letters.
4. Each student saves his or her file to a diskette.
5. Students send the diskettes to their pen pals. The pen pal reads the letter and responds by adding to the file.

Evaluation

Select an appropriate evaluation form provided in appendix A.

Teacher's Notes

Dates: _____

Word-processing skills that need improvement: _____

_____

Remarks: _____

_____

_____

_____

_____

From *Technology Across the Curriculum.* © 1997. Marilyn J. Bazeli and James L. Heintz. Teacher Ideas Press. (800) 237-6124.

What's It Like?

Objective
Eighth-grade students enter questions into a word-processing file to ask high school students what it is like being in high school.

Overview
Eighth-grade students often have many questions about high school. This activity allows students to ask questions of high school students without peer pressure and in complete confidence. This might also serve as a writing activity for high school students.

Skill Areas
Written Communication, Word Processing

Materials Checklist
- ☐ Word-processing software
- ☐ Diskettes (one for each student)

Adaptive Ideas
This format might be used at any level in which a cooperative arrangement is possible.

Procedures
1. Set up a cooperative arrangement between two classes, especially at different grade or age levels. Eighth-grade students definitely have many questions about what it is like in high school. The high school class involved should use this as an opportunity to write concise and clear responses.
2. The eighth-grade students compose questions using word-processing software. Each student saves his or her questions to a file on a diskette.
3. Label the diskettes by a number code instead of by name to provide confidentiality for the eighth-grade students.
4. Give the diskettes to a high school class for response to the questions. The answers are saved to the same file on the diskette and then returned to the eighth-grade class.
5. Eighth-grade students read the responses. Replies and follow-up questions are an option for further interaction.

From *Technology Across the Curriculum.* © 1997. Marilyn J. Bazeli and James L. Heintz. Teacher Ideas Press. (800) 237-6124.

Evaluation

Select an appropriate evaluation form provided in appendix A.

Teacher's Notes

Dates: _____

Classes/Teachers involved: _____

Remarks: _____

_____

_____

_____

_____

_____

From *Technology Across the Curriculum.* © 1997. Marilyn J. Bazeli and James L. Heintz. Teacher Ideas Press. (800) 237-6124.

Spelling Notebook

Objective
Students keep track of high-frequency words that are often misspelled using word-processing software, to be used as a reference.

Overview
The writing process is an integral part of today's classroom. Students often inquire about the spelling of words and often misspell high-frequency words. Students keep track of these words in a word-processing file that will be made available to all students.

Skill Areas
Spelling, Written Communication, Alphabetizing, Word Processing

Materials Checklist
☐ Word-processing software

☐ Printer

Adaptive Ideas
Older students might keep their own file of often misspelled words.

Procedures
1. Set up a word-processing file titled "Words." The word-processing software and the file should remain open, especially when the students are involved in the writing process.
2. Any word that any student finds difficult to spell is entered into the file, once the correct spelling is discovered.
3. Words are alphabetized within the file.
4. As students are involved in the writing process, the file should be used as a reference to find the spelling of words.
5. Students with advanced abilities are given the task of checking for proper spelling and correct alphabetical order.
6. Print out the list on a periodic basis to be used as a reference for those students who have difficulties in spelling.

From *Technology Across the Curriculum.* © 1997. Marilyn J. Bazeli and James L. Heintz. Teacher Ideas Press. (800) 237-6124.

Evaluation
Select an appropriate evaluation form provided in appendix A.

Teacher's Notes

Dates: _____

Remarks: _____

_____

_____

_____

_____

_____

_____

From *Technology Across the Curriculum.* © 1997. Marilyn J. Bazeli and James L. Heintz. Teacher Ideas Press. (800) 237-6124.

Where to Find It

Objective
Students research a topic using different forms of media.

Overview
Students work in groups to research a topic using different forms of research media. Each group researches the same topic. Each group is assigned a different form of media, such as CD-ROM encyclopedias, printed encyclopedias, and books and videotapes on the subject. The groups compare and contrast the different types of research media.

Skill Areas
Research, Written Communication, Critical Analysis, Science, Social Studies, Health

Materials Checklist
- ☐ CD-ROM encyclopedias
- ☐ Set of printed encyclopedias
- ☐ Computer
- ☐ Printer
- ☐ Books on the selected subject
- ☐ Videotapes on the selected subject

Adaptive Ideas
Older students might use on-line news services, television news reports, newspapers, and weekly magazines to research a current topic.

Procedures
1. Divide students into small research groups. Assign all groups the same topic, such as the Civil War, the solar system, the circulatory system in the human body, and so on.
2. Assign each group a different media form in which to find information. Media forms should include CD-ROM encyclopedias, sets of printed encyclopedias, and books and videotapes on the subject.
3. Each group of students prepares a report using *only* the information found in the media assigned to that group.
4. Each group gives their report. Each group gives an analysis of the strengths and weaknesses of the media assigned to their group.

Evaluation

Select an appropriate evaluation form provided in appendix A. Observations noted during discussion of strength/weaknesses of various media should be assessed for critical-thinking quality.

Teacher's Notes

Dates: _____

Types of media used: _____

Remarks: _____

_____

_____

_____

_____

_____

From *Technology Across the Curriculum.* © 1997. Marilyn J. Bazeli and James L. Heintz. Teacher Ideas Press. (800) 237-6124.

Map the Way

Objective
Students use a computer-based encyclopedia to discover related topics and how they interrelate.

Overview
Small groups of students investigate a given topic in science, social studies, or health. Each group uses a computer-based encyclopedia to investigate the topic. Each group searches the related areas and creates a map of how the areas interrelate.

Skill Areas
Research, Social Studies, Science, Health

Materials Checklist
☐ CD-ROM encyclopedia

Adaptive Ideas
Younger students might be guided by the teacher, each day examining a related topic.

Procedures
1. Divide the class into small groups to perform research using a CD-ROM encyclopedia.
2. Assign each group a broad topic, such as the human body, World War II, mammals, and so on.
3. Students record and map out all the related paths of the main topic.
4. The related topics are explored to find any further extension of the main topic.
5. Each group diagrams the related research structure of the main topic. The mapping may be done by charting—creating a web of interrelated topics on a flowchart diagram.
6. Each group presents a discussion of how the related topics are connected to the main topic.

From *Technology Across the Curriculum.* © 1997. Marilyn J. Bazeli and James L. Heintz. Teacher Ideas Press. (800) 237-6124.

Evaluation

Select an appropriate evaluation form provided in appendix A.

For Portfolios:

☐ Photocopy the flowchart diagram of each student.

Teacher's Notes

Dates: _____

Type of CD-ROM used: _____

Remarks: _____

_____

_____

_____

_____

_____

From *Technology Across the Curriculum.* © 1997. Marilyn J. Bazeli and James L. Heintz. Teacher Ideas Press. (800) 237-6124.

Go Find the Grammar

Objective
Students correct a set of word-processed files that contain grammatical mistakes.

Overview
This activity is designed to help students improve their grammar and proofreading skills. Small groups of students or individuals open each word-processing file, correct the paragraphs, and print out the results. Each paragraph will contain errors in punctuation, capitalization, plurals, and sentence structure.

Skill Areas
English, Proofreading, Word Processing

Materials Checklist
- ☐ Word-processing software
- ☐ Text files on diskette (see "Procedures")
- ☐ Printer

Adaptive Ideas
Older students might use word-processing tools, such as spell checkers and grammar checkers, to correct the paragraphs.

Procedures
1. Prepare a set of word-processed paragraphs saved in separate files. Each paragraph should contain mistakes in capitalization, punctuation, plurals and singular form, and subject/verb agreement. The files should be sequenced in order of difficulty. The files should be write-protected.
2. Students working in small groups or individually open a file and correct the mistakes by proofreading the paragraph and then entering the changes. The file is printed out for evaluation.
3. Students meet with the teacher to assess the mistakes that were corrected. Problem areas are discussed and remedied.
4. Students continue to work through the set of files. (Teachers might wish to have a set of remedial files for those students requiring additional practice.)

From *Technology Across the Curriculum*. © 1997. Marilyn J. Bazeli and James L. Heintz. Teacher Ideas Press. (800) 237-6124.

Evaluation

Evaluation of the objective should be done in individual and group conferences.

Teacher's Notes

Dates: _____

Types of grammatical mistakes used: _____

_____

Remarks: _____

_____

_____

_____

_____

From *Technology Across the Curriculum.* © 1997. Marilyn J. Bazeli and James L. Heintz. Teacher Ideas Press. (800) 237-6124.

Chapter 6
Multimedia Productions

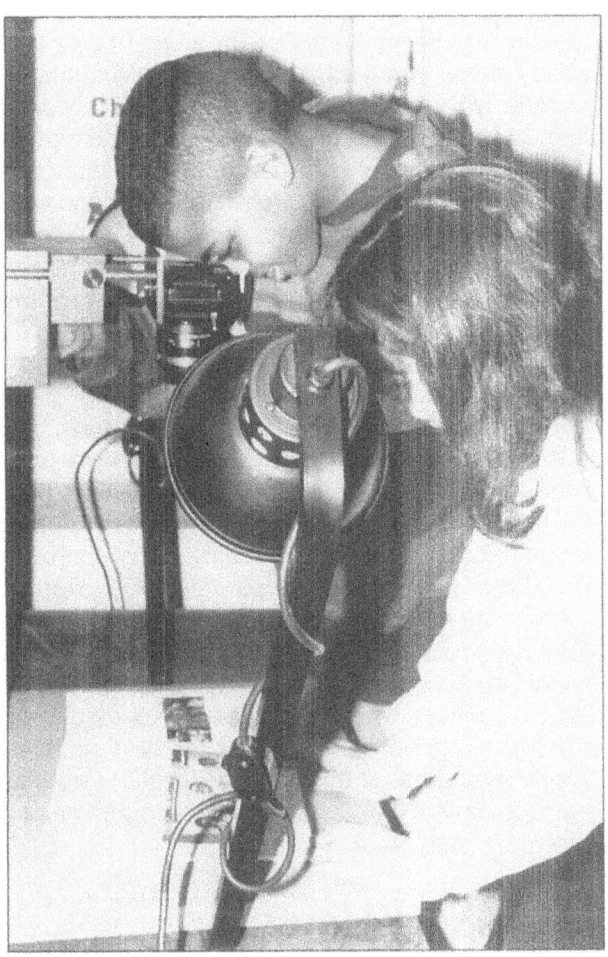

THE TERM *multimedia* has been defined as "the sequential or simultaneous use of a variety of media formats in a given presentation or self-study program," and a multimedia system is "a combination of audio and visual media integrated into a structured, systematic presentation" (Heinich, Molenda, Russell, and Smaldino, 1996, p. 413). This chapter covers various media with which students are familiar, such as video, slides, sound, charts, pictures, drawings, and diagrams.

A current understanding of the definition of multimedia involves computer-controlled use of various media, such as CD-ROM, videodisc, and computer text (Agnew, Kellerman, and Meyer, 1996). However, this chapter covers curricular applications for student-produced multimedia presentations rather than the operation of the media. There are many books available today that deal directly with how to produce computer-controlled multimedia packages, which provide excellent knowledge for teachers interested in pursuing this type of production. The curricular applications for the activities described in this chapter are appropriate for the selected media as well as for more sophisticated media. As more sophisticated media become available in schools, and teachers and students become familiar with them, these media can easily be substituted for the media types selected for inclusion in these activities. The selection of media is not as important as the qualities of the media and their purpose within the curricular learning experiences of the students.

We know that learners remember more when learning involves more than one sense. The British Audiovisual Association (1983) reports that we retain 20 percent of what we hear, 30 percent of what we see, and 50 percent of what we see and hear. However, we do not, as educators, effectively help students to analyze the specific qualities of visuals and sound and their effect on learning.

Critical thinking can be developed in students when they become involved with analyzing, in terms of communication and learning, the effect of removing one element from a multimedia production. As each individual element is analyzed on its own merits, students become better able to analyze the effect of the entire multimedia production on communication and learning. For example, turning off the sound during a battle in a Star Wars movie, and even substituting it with soft, sweet music, gives a completely different feel to the production. Students need to have these kinds of comparisons to understand more sophisticated multimedia packages involving sound, motion, still photography, and so on. Each element, as it has been presented in previous chapters in this book, has merits and advantages of its own. Only when students have worked with each individual medium can they correctly create effective multimedia productions.

Selecting several media and combining them into one presentation involves knowledge of not only the individual media but also of how they might fit together. For example, pictures, charts, graphs, drawings, and other still visuals have the advantage of being seen over time. Motion visuals, such as film, video, and some computer programs, have the advantage of motion but the disadvantage of a short viewing time. If still visuals are to be combined with motion visuals in a multimedia production, the advantages and limitations of each need to be considered.

Creating a multimedia project gives students opportunities to learn academic subjects while becoming involved in the exciting use of several media to express information (Agnew, Kellerman, and Meyer, 1996). "The five useful media are text, graphics, images, audio, and video" (p. 2). While using combinations of some or all of these media, students learn to organize media and to achieve academic goals.

In this chapter, the activities described involve students in organizing/producing or analyzing multimedia productions. Familiar media that are among the five useful media described by Agnew, Kellerman, and Meyer (1996) for multimedia productions have been selected for inclusion. This enables students to focus on their learning rather than on mastering a new medium. As explained previously, these activities do not include computer-controlled multimedia presentation tools such as HyperCard, LinkWay, and Authorware. However, many of the activities described here can easily be adapted to computer-controlled systems involving videodisc players rather than slides, a digital camera rather than slide film/camera, and computer-generated charts/diagrams rather than student-drawn charts/diagrams. Again, it is not the media that are important, but rather how they are used to engage students actively in learning, to promote critical-viewing and critical-thinking skills, and to prepare students to be lifelong learners.

Extracurricular Activity— "Community Multimedia Show"

Students enjoy and become very motivated producing multimedia productions. When they know that their productions will be part of a community show, they become even more accountable for their learning and presentation. One class used their various skills to take pictures and make posters, promoting an evening "Community Multimedia Show" at the school. A small admission was charged, and student productions were set up in various areas and rooms of the school. Community members, parents, and friends moved from location to location, viewing the multimedia productions on display. The students used the admission fees to treat themselves to a pizza party and buy more video and audio tapes for future productions. The public relations results from the evening were even more rewarding; additionally, local business people discussed the possibility of increased support for the school. It was expressed by many people in attendance that community members too often do not have such an opportunity to view quality work done by students, in connection with specific curricular areas. Oftentimes, science fairs or history fairs are places where student work is displayed, but frequently only the work of the best students. The presentations at this multimedia show were by every student in the class, and the community members were impressed!

References

Agnew, P., A. Kellerman, and J. Meyer. 1996. *Multimedia in the classroom*. Boston: Allyn & Bacon.

British Audiovisual Association. 1983. Report, as quoted in *InteractiveVideo*, edited by Eric Parsloe and researched by Signe Hoffos and the EPIC Team. Cheshire, U.K.: Sigma Technical Press.

Heinich, R., M. Molenda, J. Russell, and S. Smaldino. 1996. *Instructional media and technologies for learning*. Englewood Cliffs, NJ: Prentice-Hall.

More Ideas

Curricular Areas **Production Ideas**

From *Technology Across the Curriculum.* © 1997. Marilyn J. Bazeli and James L. Heintz. Teacher Ideas Press. (800) 237-6124.

Activities

Slide/Tape Production: Curricular Areas

Objective
Students produce a slide show with taped narration to accompany their study of any curricular area.

Overview
In connection with any topic being studied in class, students take slides (either live or of pictures in books using a copystand) and then write a script to accompany the slides. After practicing the script, and using music if desired, students record the narration on a tape recorder.

Skill Areas
All Curricular Areas (particularly English)

Materials Checklist
- ☐ Camera
- ☐ Slide film
- ☐ Tape recorder
- ☐ Audio tape
- ☐ Resource materials as necessary
- ☐ Slide projector with carousel for slides

Adaptive Ideas
Younger children might be required to produce a short number of slides (five or six), while older children should produce a much longer presentation.

This activity can easily be adapted to any curricular area, and would enhance visual skills of the students by involving them in locating pictures or real-life situations for the slides.

Procedures
1. Begin with a discussion of topic areas within the general unit being studied in a curricular area. Students either select or are assigned a topic area to work on.
2. Individually or in cooperative groups, students decide upon visuals that might depict what they want to show in their particular topic.
3. Students decide whether they take a live picture of each visual, or whether they need to locate a picture of the desired visual in a book or other source material. If they choose live pictures, guidelines for effective photographs should be discussed (see the introduction to chapter 3). If they choose to select a visual in a book, they will use a copystand (see appendix C for equipment description and instructions).
4. Students take the pictures, using slide film, and the teacher has the slide film developed.

From *Technology Across the Curriculum.* © 1997. Marilyn J. Bazeli and James L. Heintz. Teacher Ideas Press. (800) 237-6124.

5. When the slides are available, students review their slides and, using a storyboard, decide upon the order for the slides and the type of script (see appendix B for scriptwriting guidelines and storyboard forms).
6. Students write their scripts. This can be accomplished by individual effort, group work, or each person within a group taking responsibility for designated slides.
7. Students practice the script, with emphasis placed on clear pronunciation, and pauses used when slides are changed.
8. Students decide whether music is desired at the beginning and/or end of the recorded presentation.
9. Students record the presentation with a tape recorder, making sure that the surroundings are as quiet as possible.
10. Present the finished sound/slide production to the class.

Evaluation

Select an appropriate evaluation form provided in appendix A.

Student work can be evaluated in several ways:
- English—mechanics of the script
- Oral presentation skills
- Appropriate selection of visuals related to the topic
- Appropriate description of the visuals, as related to the topic

For Portfolios:

☐ Photocopy the written script of each student.

Teacher's Notes

Dates: _____

Topics: _____

Comments: _____

_____

_____

_____

_____

_____

From *Technology Across the Curriculum.* © 1997. Marilyn J. Bazeli and James L. Heintz. Teacher Ideas Press. (800) 237-6124.

Slide/Tape Production: Visual Analysis Activity

Objective
Students write a creative script to accompany a specific set of slides.

Overview
The teacher selects a set of slides (a specific theme or unrelated). The students are required to create a script for these slides, uniting them into a logical sequence and treatment.

Skill Areas
Visual Literacy, English, Creative Writing

Materials Checklist
- ☐ Tape recorder
- ☐ Slide projector with carousel for slides
- ☐ Optional: Audio cassette of music and another tape player

Adaptive Ideas
This activity works best when groups of students work together, discussing the treatment for their script and the order of the slides. The actual writing of the script can be done either in the group setting or by individuals within the group. If individuals write parts of the script, they must all agree cooperatively on the final product.

Procedures
1. Begin with a presentation on scriptwriting. This can be a brief guide for scriptwriting, or a more detailed lesson on scripting techniques (see appendix B for guidelines).
2. Show the selected group of slides (this can be any number, but it is best to start with no more than 10, and less for younger students). Students can be required to use *all* of the slides, or they can be allowed the choice of using any 8 of the 10 slides, and so on.
3. In groups, students decide what treatment they want to use for their script. Next, they decide on the sequence of the slides for their production.
4. Students then write their script, either as a group or individually, using a storyboard (see appendix B for storyboard forms). The final script is shared with the group and then practiced together.
5. Within each group, students can critique each other in terms of clarity of speech, expression, needed inflection, and so on, as appropriate for their group script.
6. If music is desired, the students practice playing the music at the desired times, with fade-in and fade-out techniques also practiced.
7. Students record the final scripts.

From *Technology Across the Curriculum.* © 1997. Marilyn J. Bazeli and James L. Heintz. Teacher Ideas Press. (800) 237-6124.

8. Each group shares their completed script with the class. A class discussion should be conducted, including:

   various interpretations of the slides by different groups

   possible reasons for varied interpretations

   which slides were consistently rejected (if students were allowed to reject one or two slides)

   how people see things differently, and derive different meanings from the same visuals

   implications for everyday visuals, such as news, television shows, different views of witnesses to accidents, illustrations in books, and so on

Evaluation

The scripts might be evaluated for writing skills. The presentation skills of each group member might also be evaluated. Cooperative skills are important in this activity, and might be a part of the evaluation of the success of the activity. See appendix A for possible evaluation forms.

Teacher's Notes

Dates: _____

Slides used: _____

Comments: _____

_____

_____

_____

_____

_____

From *Technology Across the Curriculum.* © 1997. Marilyn J. Bazeli and James L. Heintz. Teacher Ideas Press. (800) 237-6124.

Slide/Tape Production: Special Events

Objective
To preserve a visual and verbal record of special classroom events.

Overview
Students take 6 to 12 slides of a special event, such as a guest speaker, field trip, holiday celebration, program for parents, and so on. Students write a script describing the event and record the script. By the end of the year, a slide/tape collection will document special events that occurred during the school year.

Skill Areas
Writing, Presentation

Materials Checklist
- ☐ Camera
- ☐ Slide film
- ☐ Tape recorder
- ☐ Slide projector with carousel for slides
- ☐ Audio cassette for music
- ☐ Optional: Second tape player

Adaptive Ideas
Different groups of students could be assigned to different classroom events so that, by the end of the semester or year, all students will have been involved in this activity, but not at the same time.

Procedures
1. As a special classroom event approaches, assign a specific student or small group of students to be responsible for taking slide pictures of important elements of that event. State the number of slides that can be taken (example: 8–10) so that the students have a limit and therefore plan more carefully the elements they choose to photograph. A range rather than a finite number of slides is usually necessary to allow for unplanned extra ideas.

2. Discuss guidelines for effective photographs (see the introduction to chapter 3). Discuss the necessity of taking the slides without interrupting the special event and techniques for doing this (such as standing to the side, taking posed pictures before or after the event, etc.).

3. After the slides are developed, the students write a script for the slides, giving verbal description for the event. (A variation could be that one student or small group of students takes the slides, and another student or small group writes the script for the slides. This would involve more students in one event.) See appendix B for scriptwriting guidelines and storyboard forms.

From *Technology Across the Curriculum.* © 1997. Marilyn J. Bazeli and James L. Heintz. Teacher Ideas Press. (800) 237-6124.

4. The script is practiced and recorded by the student(s) who wrote it. If desired, music may be added at the beginning or end by using a second tape player.
5. Present the final production to the class, parents, other classes, and so on. Add the video to the year-long collection of slide/tape documentations of special events.

Evaluation

Select an appropriate evaluation form in appendix A. Students might be evaluated for their writing skills and presentation skills. Also, choice of elements of the special event to photograph might be noted.

For Portfolios:

☐ Photocopy the scripts.

Teacher's Notes

Dates: _____

Events: _____

Students taking slides: _____

Students writing scripts: _____

Comments: _____

_____

_____

_____

From *Technology Across the Curriculum.* © 1997. Marilyn J. Bazeli and James L. Heintz. Teacher Ideas Press. (800) 237-6124.

162 / Chapter 6: Multimedia Productions

Filmstrip/Sound: Old Pictures, New Script

Objective
To make use of old filmstrips, students write a new script of their own to accompany the filmstrip.

Overview
Instead of throwing away old filmstrips, they can be recycled by providing the focus for a writing activity for students. Students write the script as a story, as a description of the pictures within a particular subject area, or any other creative treatment they or the teacher desire.

Skill Areas
Creative Writing (or a subject area appropriate to the pictures on the filmstrip)

Materials Checklist
- ☐ Filmstrip
- ☐ Tape recorder
- ☐ Filmstrip projector
- ☐ Optional: Audio cassette for music, and a second tape player

Adaptive Ideas
Younger children might use only part of the filmstrip for writing a shorter script. An interesting idea for older students might be to divide the filmstrip into sections, and have different groups of students write a script for each section; all sections are put together to create a new interpretation of the filmstrip.

Procedures
1. Select a filmstrip to use for this activity based on the focus. For example, if creative writing is the focus, select a filmstrip that depicts visuals about which a story could be written. If science is the focus, select a filmstrip about which students could demonstrate knowledge of the topic in their script.
2. Assign the entire project to one group of students, or parts of the filmstrip to different groups, or one designated part of the filmstrip to one group of students.
3. Students write a script to accompany the pictures on the filmstrip. See appendix B for scriptwriting guidelines and storyboard forms.
4. Students practice and record their script.
5. Present the filmstrip/sound production to the class. Feedback in discussion could be provided in terms of the accuracy of information in the script (for a particular subject area) or the elements of a story told in the script.

From *Technology Across the Curriculum.* © 1997. Marilyn J. Bazeli and James L. Heintz. Teacher Ideas Press. (800) 237-6124.

Evaluation

Select an appropriate evaluation form provided in appendix A. Student work might be evaluated for writing skills and presentation skills. In addition, if the script was written in a particular subject area, the factual information researched and given could be evaluated. If the script was written to tell a story, that story could be evaluated in terms of elements studied in class, such as characters, setting, beginning, middle, end of story, and so on.

For Portfolios:

☐ Photocopy the scripts.

Teacher's Notes

Dates: _____

Filmstrips used: _____

Focus of scripts for each filmstrip: _____

Comments: _____
_____
_____
_____
_____

Filmstrip/Sound: New Pictures, Old Script

Objective
Students make use of old filmstrip narrations. Students can use the original soundtrack, but create new, up-to-date visuals.

Overview
Sometimes older filmstrips contain visuals that look very much out-of-date, or the visuals are colorless or scratched. Instead of throwing away these filmstrips, students can be engaged in an excellent activity to create new visuals to fit with the prerecorded audio cassette. The visual that students select to photograph must complement the description of a scene on the tape. After selecting pictures to represent, students make slides of these pictures, which are then shown along with the former filmstrip's soundtrack.

Skill Areas
Visual Literacy, Critical Thinking, Problem Solving

Materials Checklist
- ☐ Camera
- ☐ Slide film
- ☐ Slide projector with carousel for slides
- ☐ Reference materials with pictures

Adaptive Ideas
This activity is best suited for older students. However, younger students might be given a short tape made by the teacher explaining rather specific visuals (perhaps only four or five).

The audio tape might be divided into sections, and different groups of students would be responsible for representing these sections visually.

Procedures
1. Select a soundtrack for use in this activity, and decide whether one group of students will work on the entire tape or groups of students will work on sections. (It would be helpful to re-record each section of the original tape to give to the group working on that section.)
2. Students use reference materials to locate appropriate visuals to accompany the script.
3. Students take slides of the visuals selected using a copystand (see appendix C for equipment description).
4. If possible, take pictures (to use for slides) of real-life scenery, people, objects, and so on (see guidelines for effective photographs in the introduction to chapter 3).

From *Technology Across the Curriculum.* © 1997. Marilyn J. Bazeli and James L. Heintz. Teacher Ideas Press. (800) 237-6124.

5. Students practice orchestrating their slides with the soundtrack.
6. Present the final production to the class.

Evaluation

Select an appropriate evaluation form provided in appendix A. Students should be evaluated on their choice of visuals and how well they accompany the original recorded script.

Teacher's Notes

Dates: _____

Filmstrip audio cassette used: _____

Reference materials located and used: _____

Comments: _____

_____

_____

_____

_____

From *Technology Across the Curriculum.* © 1997. Marilyn J. Bazeli and James L. Heintz. Teacher Ideas Press. (800) 237-6124.

Filmstrip/Sound: New Pictures, New Script

Objective
Students make use of old, unusable filmstrips by creating new pictures and scripts.

Overview
When filmstrips become unusable in terms of their visual use, they can be bleached to remove the original image. Students use the roll of clear film to draw their own simple pictures using colored markers, which will accompany their own script.

Skill Areas
All Curricular Areas (particularly Creative Writing)

Materials Checklist
- ☐ Old filmstrip (teacher will bleach to remove old images)
- ☐ Colored markers for transparencies (permanent or washable)
- ☐ Tape recorder
- ☐ Audio cassette
- ☐ Filmstrip projector
- ☐ Optional: Audio cassette of music, and a second tape player

Adaptive Ideas
Younger children might have difficulty drawing on the filmstrip because of lesser-developed eye-hand coordination. However, very simple drawings can be accomplished.

The filmstrips can be cut into any length desired. Older students should use a longer filmstrip for more visual and script creations.

Procedures
1. The teacher soaks the old filmstrips in bleach at home. (For safety reasons, do not do this in the classroom.) When the old images are no longer visible, rinse and dry the filmstrips.
2. Decide whether students will work on this project individually or in groups. (This activity usually works best individually, but students might work on segments of a filmstrip and put these together into a group production.)
3. The teacher assigns, or the student selects, a script focus for a particular subject area or writing assignment topic.
4. The student writes the script (see guidelines and storyboards in appendix B) and then draws pictures on the blank filmstrip with markers.

5. The student practices the script while viewing the filmstrip, to check for appropriate sequence and flow.
6. The student records the script on audio cassette, adding music if desired.
7. The student presents the completed filmstrip and accompanying audio cassette to the class.

Evaluation

Select an evaluation form provided in appendix A. Students might be evaluated for the appropriateness of the script for the chosen or assigned topic. The writing skills demonstrated in the script might be part of the evaluation.

For Portfolios:

☐ Photocopy the written script of each student.

Teacher's Notes

Dates: _____

Topic of production: _____

Comments/Ideas: _____

_____

_____

_____

_____

_____

From *Technology Across the Curriculum.* © 1997. Marilyn J. Bazeli and James L. Heintz. Teacher Ideas Press. (800) 237-6124.

Slides/Video/Sound: Community, Past and Present

Objective
Students create a visual presentation of their community using photographs from the past combined with a video of the present.

Overview
Students use old photographs of community scenes, new videotape of current scenes, and recorded narration to orchestrate a portrait of their community.

Skill Areas
Social Studies, History, Written Communication

Materials Checklist
- ☐ Camera with macro lens
- ☐ Copystand (see appendix C for equipment description)
- ☐ Slide film
- ☐ Video camera and tape
- ☐ Tape recorder and audio cassette
- ☐ Slide projector with carousel for slides
- ☐ VCR and monitor
- ☐ Optional: Audio cassette of music and a second tape player

Adaptive Ideas
Because of the various media involved in this activity, younger children will need adult assistance.

Procedures
1. Individually or in groups, students discuss and decide upon a theme for a historical presentation of their community. A theme might be businesses in the community, schools, homes, people, and so on.
2. Students locate old pictures to depict the historical background of the theme. For example, photographs of the downtown area at various stages through the past would show the development of the businesses in the community.
3. Using a camera with slide film and a copystand, students take slides of the old photographs (see appendix C for equipment description).
4. A video camera is used to show current visuals regarding the chosen theme within the community. For example, the current downtown area could be videotaped, with careful representation of old buildings with new interiors, new buildings, or new businesses.

From *Technology Across the Curriculum.* © 1997. Marilyn J. Bazeli and James L. Heintz. Teacher Ideas Press. (800) 237-6124.

5. Students write a script to narrate the older photographs in appropriate sequence, ending with narration for the video scenes of the present day (see appendix B for scriptwriting guidelines).
6. Students videotape the slides as they are projected.
7. Students combine the videotape of slides and the live videotape, with audio added, by using several VCRs and a microphone (see appendix C for specific instructions). Use video editing equipment (if available) to create a more professional production. If desired, record music (at the beginning, end, or quietly throughout the presentation) to accompany the script.
8. Share this presentation with community groups as well as the school.

Evaluation

Select an evaluation form provided in appendix A. Research in social studies and history might be evaluated in terms of accuracy and completeness. Writing skills, as demonstrated in the script, might also be evaluated.

For Portfolios:

☐ Make a copy of the videotape.

Teacher's Notes

Dates: _____

Themes: _____

Comments/Ideas for future use: _____

_____

_____

_____

_____

_____

From *Technology Across the Curriculum.* © 1997. Marilyn J. Bazeli and James L. Heintz. Teacher Ideas Press. (800) 237-6124.

Slides/Video/Sound: Family History

Objective
Students document their family history using photographs and videotape.

Overview
Students select photographs of their ancestors to make into slides and videotape current family members. A script is written to accompany the photos and video clips. The result is a visual family timeline or family tree.

Skill Areas
Social Studies, Writing

Materials Checklist
- [ ] Camera with macro lens
- [ ] Copystand (see appendix C for equipment description)
- [ ] Slide film
- [ ] Video camera and tape
- [ ] Microphone for camera
- [ ] Slide projector with carousel for slides
- [ ] VCR and TV
- [ ] Optional: Tape recorder and audio cassette with music

Adaptive Ideas
Younger children will need a great deal of adult assistance to complete this project. However, limiting the number of photographs used will make the project shorter and easier to complete. Also, focusing on one particular member of the family, such as a grandmother, will make the project easier for younger children to accomplish.

Procedures
1. Students select one or more members of their family to represent in their project.
2. Students gather old photographs.
3. Students take slides of the old photographs, using a copystand (see appendix C for equipment description).
4. Students write a script to narrate the slides (see appendix B for scriptwriting guidelines and storyboards).
5. Students videotape slides while they are projected, with accompanying narration.

6. Students write interview questions for living family members and show the questions to the interviewees before videotaping.
7. Using a video camera with microphone, students interview family members, recording the actual interview on videotape (the microphone provides better sound quality).
8. Students combine the videotape of slides and the videotape of family interviews into one tape using a second VCR to dub each, in proper sequence. (Editing equipment can be used for a more professional presentation.)

Evaluation

Select an appropriate evaluation form provided in appendix A. Students might be evaluated on their writing skills and their historical representation of their family.

For Portfolios:

☐ Make a copy of the videotape.

Teacher's Notes

Dates: _____

Comments/Ideas for future use: _____

_____

_____

_____

_____

_____

From *Technology Across the Curriculum.* © 1997. Marilyn J. Bazeli and James L. Heintz. Teacher Ideas Press. (800) 237-6124.

Slides/Video/Sound: Videotape Slide Productions

Objective
Students make slide productions easier to use by making them into videotapes.

Overview
Slide productions are sometimes difficult to present because of the amount of equipment involved, especially if a soundtrack accompanies the slides. However, videotaping the slide production provides a quick and easy solution.

Skill Areas
Various Curricular Areas

Materials Checklist
- ☐ Slide projector with carousel for slides
- ☐ Tape player (if the script has been previously recorded)
- ☐ Slides (and audio cassette) of previously produced slide presentation
- ☐ Video camera and tripod

Adaptive Ideas
This is mainly an activity for teachers, to provide ease of use for student-produced slide presentations. However, older children can do this activity with guidance.

After videotaping the slide production, it is suggested that the original slide production be retained because, for large groups, it is still more effective to use the slides rather than the videotape.

Procedures
1. Set up the slide projector four to five feet from the screen, so that the projected image is fairly small and extremely clear.
2. If the script has been previously recorded, set up the tape recorder nearby.
3. Attach the video camera to the tripod and set up directly behind and above the slide projector.
4. Run the slide/sound production, and videotape it simultaneously. (To avoid the sound of the slides changing, run a microphone from the video camera some distance away, and place the tape recorder at that location.)

Evaluation

None.

For Portfolios:

☐ Make a copy of the videotape.

Teacher's Notes

Dates: _____

Slide productions on videotape: _____

Ideas/Comments: _____

_____

_____

_____

_____

_____

From *Technology Across the Curriculum.* © 1997. Marilyn J. Bazeli and James L. Heintz. Teacher Ideas Press. (800) 237-6124.

Video/Sound: Television Without Sound

Objective
To encourage critical thinking and comprehension of what is *seen*, students view a television clip without sound.

Overview
Students in today's visual world need many opportunities to develop critical thinking regarding the media. This activity, which is teacher-produced and teacher-led, encourages and guides students to apply critical-thinking skills to images on television. A television clip is shown, without sound, and students discuss the meaning of the sequence.

Skill Areas
Critical Thinking, Problem Solving

Materials Checklist

- [ ] VCR at home or school to tape segments of television shows

  or

- [ ] Videotapes in a school library, from which segments can be viewed

- [ ] VCR and monitor in the classroom

Adaptive Ideas
The length of the segment shown should depend upon the age of the students. Also, the depth of discussion regarding the comprehension of the segment when only the visual is used should vary with age groups and maturity of the students.

Though this activity is designed for an entire class, it can also be adapted for small groups. After viewing the video clip, students might break into small groups to discuss the meaning of the clip, write a consensus description, and then reassemble for a class discussion.

This activity might be done in reverse; that is, play only the *sound* of a video clip and then discuss comprehension of the segment.

Procedures
1. Select a portion of a television show to tape for use in this activity, or select a portion of a videotape from the school library.
2. Preview the selected clip, without sound, to make sure it is suitable for this activity. For example, is it possible to comprehend some of the story or the information, or is the clip too abstract? For older students, more abstraction is useful for comparing what is *seen* to what the total presentation, with sound and visuals, depicts.

From *Technology Across the Curriculum.* © 1997. Marilyn J. Bazeli and James L. Heintz. Teacher Ideas Press. (800) 237-6124.

3. Begin the class lesson with a discussion of television being a multimedia production, involving both sound and visuals to tell a story or present information. Explain the activity to the students, telling them that they will be using only their sense of sight to determine the story or information being presented, and that they must use critical-thinking skills to comprehend the action.

4. Show the television clip.

5. Open and lead a discussion about action in the clip.

6. After considerable discussion (hopefully with varying thoughts about the meaning), show the clip again with sound. Discuss how comprehension changes when sound is added to the visual. Guide students to the realization that we often need more than one of our senses to interpret and understand a situation correctly.

7. If desired, reverse this activity; that is, show another clip, using only the sound. Again, the purpose is to help students think about what we hear and the importance of gaining information through several senses when trying to comprehend a given situation.

Evaluation

The quality of discussion will provide evaluative information on the development of students' critical-thinking abilities and the level of success of the lesson.

Teacher's Notes

Dates: _____

Segments used: _____

Observations on quality of discussion: _____

Comments: _____

_____

_____

_____

_____

From *Technology Across the Curriculum.* © 1997. Marilyn J. Bazeli and James L. Heintz. Teacher Ideas Press. (800) 237-6124.

Video/Sound: Television, Critical Thinking, and Sequence

Objective
Students develop critical-thinking skills regarding sequencing a series of events.

Overview
Students are shown segments of a television show, out of order. Students attempt to determine the correct sequence of these segments.

Skill Areas
Critical Thinking, Problem Solving

Materials Checklist
- ☐ VCR at home or school, to videotape segments of a television show

    or
- ☐ School library videotape
- ☐ VCR and monitor in the classroom

Adaptive Ideas
This is a teacher-produced and teacher-led activity. However, older students can videotape and present segments of a television show out of order and lead the class to determine the correct order.

Procedures
1. Select a television show or a short videotape that presents a story.
2. Videotape various segments of the story, allowing blank footage between each segment to separate the segments.
3. Begin the lesson with a discussion of sequence. Listing steps involved in a familiar process, such as hitting a baseball, will be helpful. Apply the concept of sequence to stories and television shows. Tell the students that they will be looking at events in a television show that are out of sequence, and that they will need to think to put them into the correct sequence.
4. Show the out-of-sequence videotape.
5. Lead a discussion of clues that students observed and their ideas regarding the correct order of the segments.
6. After many observations and ideas are discussed, show the correct order (or the entire show or videotape if it is short enough) to allow students to check and evaluate their critical-viewing and critical-thinking skills.

From *Technology Across the Curriculum*. © 1997. Marilyn J. Bazeli and James L. Heintz. Teacher Ideas Press. (800) 237-6124.

Evaluation

Noting the amount of observations and clues discussed by the students, and the quality of discussion, will provide evaluative information regarding the students' critical-viewing and critical-thinking skills. If this activity is repeated periodically throughout a school year, continued observation and noting of students' critical-thinking skills as demonstrated in discussions will provide developmental evaluative information.

Teacher's Notes

Dates: _____

Television shows used: _____

Videotapes used: _____

Comments: _____

_____

_____

_____

_____

From *Technology Across the Curriculum.* © 1997. Marilyn J. Bazeli and James L. Heintz. Teacher Ideas Press. (800) 237-6124.

Video/Sound/Graphics: Produce an Instructional Video

Objective
Students apply logical and sequential thinking skills to a curricular topic to produce an effective instructional video.

Overview
Students select a particular topic within the curriculum. They analyze the topic; list instructional steps in a logical and sequential manner; develop charts, graphs, pictures, and so on to illustrate the topic; and then write a script to teach the topic using the format of an instructional video.

Skill Areas
Critical Thinking, All Curricular Areas

Materials Checklist
- ☐ Reference materials
- ☐ Poster board, markers, chalkboard, and so on for creating visuals
- ☐ Video camera

Adaptive Ideas
Sometimes students learn best when a peer explains a process or concept to them. Also, students learn when they become involved in explaining the topic to another person. This activity can be done with all age groups, with topics appropriate to their learning level.

Procedures
1. Begin with the presentation of guidelines for designing instruction. These guidelines might include:
   - At the beginning, tell the audience what they will be learning to do (state the objective). Try to grab the attention and motivation of the audience.
   - Analyze the overall objective and list in order each piece of information or each task the learners need to learn or do.
   - Create any visuals, such as charts or drawings, that would help in the instruction.
   - End by reviewing the steps that were presented in the instruction (the steps could be listed on a chart). Closing statements, such as encouraging the audience or hoping for success, provide closure to the lesson.
   - Practice and try out the instruction.
2. Students select or are assigned a topic to teach.

3. Individually or in groups, students carefully analyze the steps and plan their instruction. If any equipment is needed, such as a chalkboard, they should plan for that. If visuals can be created ahead of time, such as charts listing important points or diagrams to illustrate points, they should be planned and constructed.
4. Students decide on an effective introduction to get the attention of the audience and to state the learning objective. Students decide on an effective conclusion, involving the review of learning steps and closing statements.
5. The instructional lesson is practiced and tried out with one or two students. Feedback should be given by these students regarding the steps of instruction and whether anything had been left out. Students should incorporate this feedback into their final presentation.
6. Videotape the final instructional lesson.
7. Share the videotapes with other classes. Keep the videotapes in the classroom or in a learning center for other students to view.

Evaluation

Select an appropriate evaluation form provided in appendix A. Students' concepts of the topic being taught can be evaluated. Selection of appropriate visuals and presentation skills might be a secondary evaluative element.

For Portfolios:

☐ Make a copy of the video.

Teacher's Notes

Dates: _____

Topics of lessons: _____

Locations of videotaped lessons: _____

Comments/Ideas for future use: _____

_____

_____

_____

From *Technology Across the Curriculum.* © 1997. Marilyn J. Bazeli and James L. Heintz. Teacher Ideas Press. (800) 237-6124.

Videodisc: Classroom Movie Critics

Objective
Students view a movie on videodisc to develop teamwork skills and analysis/critical-thinking skills.

Overview
Students watch a movie on videodisc. Working in groups, students analyze the movie in terms of specific elements and come to a group decision regarding their opinion of the effectiveness and quality of the movie.

Skill Areas
Critical Thinking, Cooperative Learning, Media Analysis

Materials Checklist
- ☐ Videodisc player and monitor (large enough to be viewed by the entire class)
- ☐ Videodisc of a selected movie

Adaptive Ideas
For younger children, one scene from a movie would be more effective than a whole movie.

Procedures
1. Begin by discussing with the class some specific elements they could use as an initial focus for their critique. Some of these elements might include: use of visual shots and angles; use of color, music, and sound effects; sound quality; pace of events; character development; story development; effectiveness of combined sound/visuals/script; and visual depiction of characters (make-up, clothing, physical appearance). Students should be encouraged to add their own observations for critique to those discussed in class.
2. Show the movie to the class.
3. Divide the students into groups to discuss/critique the movie in terms of elements discussed in class and any other observations.
4. Each group reaches a consensus for opinions related to the evaluative elements.
5. Each group presents their opinions.
6. Hold a class discussion, based upon the group presentations, to provide additional critical-analysis opportunities for the students.

From *Technology Across the Curriculum.* © 1997. Marilyn J. Bazeli and James L. Heintz. Teacher Ideas Press. (800) 237-6124.

Evaluation

Participation of each student within the discussion groups should be noted. Cooperative group work should be noted.

Teacher's Notes

Dates: _____

Movies viewed: _____

Comments: _____

_____

_____

_____

_____

_____

From *Technology Across the Curriculum.* © 1997. Marilyn J. Bazeli and James L. Heintz. Teacher Ideas Press. (800) 237-6124.

Videodisc: Problem-Solving Skills

Objective
Students develop problem-solving skills by viewing a movie on videodisc with pauses to discuss possible solutions to problems within the movie.

Overview
The videodisc is an effective medium for this activity because of the unique quality to locate specific segments of a movie quickly and easily. The purpose of this activity is to encourage critical thinking and problem solving by showing a segment of a movie demonstrating a problem, but stopping at the point where a solution develops. Students discuss possible solutions to the problem. Students then view the actual resolution to the problem. Discussion is conducted regarding the effectiveness and appropriateness of the actual resolution.

Skill Areas
Critical Thinking, Problem Solving

Materials Checklist
- ☐ Videodisc player and monitor (large enough to be viewed by the entire class)
- ☐ Videodisc of a selected movie

Adaptive Ideas
For older students, show an initial segment of the movie and then forward to a later segment. Students analyze what happened in the missing segment.

Procedures
1. Start a movie on videodisc to show the entire class.
2. At a predesignated spot (the teacher will need to preview the movie to select an effective part of the story, where a problem has developed), the teacher stops the videodisc.
3. Students then, either individually or in groups, describe the problem and attempt to develop possible solutions to the problem.
4. Students share the possible solutions, discuss the pros and cons of each solution, and decide upon the best solution.
5. The teacher continues the story on videodisc, so that the students can see the problem solution the writers have provided.
6. Students discuss and compare their choice(s) of the best solution with the solution that was depicted in the story.

From *Technology Across the Curriculum.* © 1997. Marilyn J. Bazeli and James L. Heintz. Teacher Ideas Press. (800) 237-6124.

Evaluation

Select an appropriate evaluation form provided in appendix A. Participation and cooperation of the students should be noted.

Teacher's Notes

Dates: _____

Movies viewed: _____

Frame number at the start of the problem: _____

Comments: _____

_____

_____

_____

_____

From *Technology Across the Curriculum*. © 1997. Marilyn J. Bazeli and James L. Heintz. Teacher Ideas Press. (800) 237-6124.

Videodisc: Analyze Characters

Objective
Students analyze specific characters and their roles in a movie, as well as the techniques used by actors to portray these characters.

Overview
The videodisc is an effective medium for this activity because of the unique quality to locate specific segments of a movie quickly and easily. The teacher leads the analysis of one specific character at a time by moving from one scene to another and engaging students in a discussion of the importance of that character to the story, the role the character has in the story, changes in the character throughout the story, and so on. In addition, students analyze specific techniques used by the actor to portray the personality of the character.

Skill Areas
Critical Thinking, Narrative Writing, Interpretation and Analysis of Literature

Materials Checklist
- [ ] Videodisc of a selected movie
- [ ] Videodisc player and monitor (large enough to be viewed by the entire class)

Adaptive Ideas
Other elements of the visual depiction of the story that might be analyzed: set design, costume design, story development, and adherence to the novel (if based on a novel).

Procedures
1. The teacher views the movie on videodisc, carefully recording frame numbers of segments that could be used in classroom discussions centering on character development or other topics (this is time-consuming, but once done, the frame locations can be used to quickly focus discussion on many different topics).
2. The teacher selects sequences to accompany the desired analysis, such as a specific character.
3. Show the desired laserdisc sequences with pauses for class discussion.

From *Technology Across the Curriculum.* © 1997. Marilyn J. Bazeli and James L. Heintz. Teacher Ideas Press. (800) 237-6124.

Evaluation

The effectiveness of this procedure can be evaluated by the ability of the students to analyze the selected element, demonstrated in either written or oral form.

Teacher's Notes

Dates: _____

Movies viewed: _____

Comments: _____

_____

_____

_____

_____

_____

From *Technology Across the Curriculum.* © 1997. Marilyn J. Bazeli and James L. Heintz. Teacher Ideas Press. (800) 237-6124.

Appendix A

Evaluation Sheets

How Was My Report?

Name _____ Group _____

Project _____ Date _____

	Student Checklist			Teacher Checklist		
	Excellent	Good	Could Improve	Excellent	Good	Could Improve
Content	☐	☐	☐	☐	☐	☐
Character Representation	☐	☐	☐	☐	☐	☐
Eye Contact	☐	☐	☐	☐	☐	☐
Voice	☐	☐	☐	☐	☐	☐
Tone	☐	☐	☐	☐	☐	☐
Volume	☐	☐	☐	☐	☐	☐
Clarity	☐	☐	☐	☐	☐	☐
Expression	☐	☐	☐	☐	☐	☐

Student Responses

I prepared for my report by _____

_____

I practiced for my report by _____

_____

I learned from this project that _____

_____

Teacher Remarks

_____

_____

_____

_____

From *Technology Across the Curriculum.* © 1997. Marilyn J. Bazeli and James L. Heintz. Teacher Ideas Press. (800) 237-6124.

How Was My Presentation?

Name _____ Group _____

Project _____ Date _____

	Student Checklist			Teacher Checklist		
	Excellent	Good	Could Improve	Excellent	Good	Could Improve
Content	☐	☐	☐	☐	☐	☐
Voice	☐	☐	☐	☐	☐	☐
Tone	☐	☐	☐	☐	☐	☐
Volume	☐	☐	☐	☐	☐	☐
Clarity of words	☐	☐	☐	☐	☐	☐
Expression	☐	☐	☐	☐	☐	☐
Enthusiasm	☐	☐	☐	☐	☐	☐
Interest in topic	☐	☐	☐	☐	☐	☐

Student Responses

I prepared for my presentation by _____

_____

I practiced for my presentation by _____

_____

I learned from this project that _____

_____

Teacher Remarks

_____

_____

_____

_____

From *Technology Across the Curriculum*. © 1997. Marilyn J. Bazeli and James L. Heintz. Teacher Ideas Press. (800) 237-6124.

Portfolio Presentation Evaluation Sheet

Name _____ Date _____

Project Description _____

_____

_____

_____

_____

What new knowledge I learned from the research of this project: _____

_____

_____

_____

_____

Research Materials Used: _____

_____

_____

_____

_____

Media Used: _____

_____

_____

_____

_____

From *Technology Across the Curriculum.* © 1997. Marilyn J. Bazeli and James L. Heintz. Teacher Ideas Press. (800) 237-6124.

Portfolio Project Evaluation Sheet

Name _____ Date _____

Project Proposal _____
_____
_____
_____
_____

Teacher Approval/Comments:

Student Evaluation of Project:

_____
_____
_____
_____

Teacher Comments:

	Excellent	Great	Good	Could Improve
Student Rating	☐	☐	☐	☐
Group Rating	☐	☐	☐	☐
Teacher Rating	☐	☐	☐	☐

From *Technology Across the Curriculum.* © 1997. Marilyn J. Bazeli and James L. Heintz. Teacher Ideas Press. (800) 237-6124.

Portfolio Project Evaluation Sheet

Name _____ Date _____

Type of Project: _____

Group Members: _____

Type of Media Used: _____

Evaluation of the Project:

Group: _____

_____

_____

Individual: _____

_____

_____

Teacher: _____

_____

_____

Parents: _____

_____

_____

From *Technology Across the Curriculum.* © 1997. Marilyn J. Bazeli and James L. Heintz. Teacher Ideas Press. (800) 237-6124.

Project Evaluation Sheet

Name _____ Date _____

Type of Project: _____

Group Members: _____

Type of Media Used: _____

Preparation   A   B   C   D   F

    Comments: _____

_____

_____

Presentation   A   B   C   D   F

    Comments: _____

_____

_____

Supporting Materials   A   B   C   D   F

    Comments: _____

_____

_____

Overall   A   B   C   D   F

    Comments: _____

_____

_____

Student Comments: _____

_____

_____

From *Technology Across the Curriculum.* © 1997. Marilyn J. Bazeli and James L. Heintz. Teacher Ideas Press. (800) 237-6124.

Assessment for Student Participation

% of Participation of Students: _____

Attitude: _____

Motivation: _____

Enthusiasm/Interest Demonstrated:

Discussion Observations:

Presentation of Finished Product:

Special Notes:

From *Technology Across the Curriculum.* © 1997. Marilyn J. Bazeli and James L. Heintz. Teacher Ideas Press. (800) 237-6124.

Observation of Class Development over Time

Project: _____

Observations: Date: _____

    Student attitudes:

    Quality of student discussions:

    Student participation in discussions:

Later Observations: Date: _____

    Student attitudes:

    Quality of student discussions:

    Student participation in discussions:

From *Technology Across the Curriculum.* © 1997. Marilyn J. Bazeli and James L. Heintz. Teacher Ideas Press. (800) 237-6124.

Creative Choices Assessment

Choice of Visuals:

Appropriateness to activity:

Completeness of visual representation:

Overall effectiveness:

Comments:

Choice of Type of Media:

Appropriateness to activity:

Completeness of visual representation:

Overall effectiveness:

Comments:

Photography:

Selection of photograph subjects:

Quality of photographs:

Explanations/captions:

Comments:

From *Technology Across the Curriculum.* © 1997. Marilyn J. Bazeli and James L. Heintz. Teacher Ideas Press. (800) 237-6124.

Appendix B

Scriptwriting Guidelines

Scriptwriting Guidelines

1. Decide on a treatment (objective).
    Examples:
    Instructional
    Informational
    Narrative
    Affective
    Promotional
    Advertisement
    Humorous

2. Use a storyboard (or index cards) to plan the visual subjects needed for the presentation.

3. Cut storyboard apart or rearrange the cards to change sequence.

4. Write a short narration for each visual subject (too many words for one visual subject creates boredom in the viewer).

5. Provide an interesting introduction to gain the interest of viewer and to establish the topic.

6. Use different voices in the narration to add variety.

7. Provide a short summary at the end, and an interesting final comment, to gain closure.

8. Music can be added, but carefully. Music can distract from the narration if it is overdone or is too loud. Usually, music is most effective at the beginning to help set the mood (fades out as the narration unfolds), and at the end to help gain closure (fades in, reaches desired volume, and fades out). Practice fading in/out techniques.

From *Technology Across the Curriculum.* © 1997. Marilyn J. Bazeli and James L. Heintz. Teacher Ideas Press. (800) 237-6124.

Dialog Guide

Project:_____

Put the name of the actor and the dialog on the spaces below. Note any movements or scene setup needed.

_____ : _____
　　　　　　　　　　　　 _____
　　　　　　　　　　　　 _____
　　　　　　　　　　　　 _____
　　　　　　　　　　　　 _____

_____ : _____
　　　　　　　　　　　　 _____
　　　　　　　　　　　　 _____
　　　　　　　　　　　　 _____
　　　　　　　　　　　　 _____

_____ : _____
　　　　　　　　　　　　 _____
　　　　　　　　　　　　 _____
　　　　　　　　　　　　 _____
　　　　　　　　　　　　 _____

_____ : _____
　　　　　　　　　　　　 _____
　　　　　　　　　　　　 _____
　　　　　　　　　　　　 _____
　　　　　　　　　　　　 _____

From *Technology Across the Curriculum*. © 1997. Marilyn J. Bazeli and James L. Heintz. Teacher Ideas Press. (800) 237-6124.

Script Guide Sheet

Sketch a picture of the frame. Write a short script to go with each frame.

Frame _____

Script _____
_____
_____
_____

Frame _____

Script _____
_____
_____
_____

Frame _____

Script _____
_____
_____
_____

Frame _____

Script _____
_____
_____
_____

From *Technology Across the Curriculum.* © 1997. Marilyn J. Bazeli and James L. Heintz. Teacher Ideas Press. (800) 237-6124.

Appendix C

Extra Equipment and Video Editing

Macro Lens

A normal lens on a 35mm camera can focus as close as 1-1/2 to 2 feet. To photograph at closer range, and especially when a copystand is being used, a macro lens is necessary. A macro lens replaces the normal camera lens. Macro lenses come in a variety of configurations, and a camera shop can help in the selection of the proper lens for use with a copystand.

Copystand

A copystand consists of a flat bed where the picture or object to be photographed is placed (1). At the back of the flat bed is a vertical post (2) on which the camera (3) is mounted, with the bottom of the camera attached to the movable holder on the post. Adjustable floodlights are attached at each side, providing bright light on the subject (4). The camera can be moved up and down on the post until the viewfinder shows the image you want. When the camera is equipped with a macro lens, close-up shots can be accomplished.

If a copystand is not available, the camera can be mounted on a tripod, and additional lighting provided.

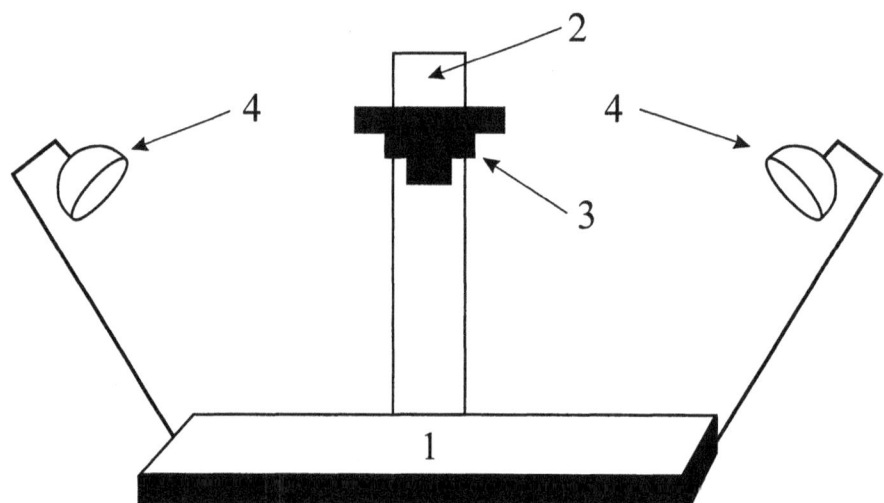

Adding a New or Different Soundtrack—Video Editing on a Shoestring

Adding a new soundtrack can be accomplished without the aid of expensive video editing devices.

Equipment Needed

2 or 3 VCR/TV setups (the camcorder can be used as a VCR/TV setup)

Camcorder

2 source videotapes

1 blank videotape

1 set of stereo cable for dubbing

Source Setup

1. Videotape the visuals on one videotape. Edit visual videotapes as necessary.
2. Prepare a script to accompany the visual presentation.
3. Set up the camcorder and position yourself to read the script while taping. The video is unimportant, so you can leave the lens cap on the camcorder.

Final Copy Procedure

1. Set up two VCR/TV combinations (A and B) to be the sources for the dubbed copy. A third VCR/TV (C) setup will record the final copy.
2. Using a dubbing cable, connect VCR-A's Video Out connection to VCR-C's Video In connection.
3. Using a dubbing cable, connect VCR-B's Audio Out connection to VCR-C's Audio In connection.
4. Place the visual tape into VCR-A, the audio tape into VCR-B, and a blank tape into VCR-C.
5. Push the PLAY buttons on VCR-A and VCR-B. As a test for the connections, you should see the picture and hear the sound on VCR-C. Rewind both tapes.
6. Push the PLAY/RECORD button on VCR-C followed by the PLAY buttons on VCR-A and VCR-B.
7. Allow tapes to record until completed.

Appendix D

Classroom Management Tips

Tip 1

Many of the activities described in this book can be done by only one group of students at a time. For example, video productions of school news can be accomplished by a different group each month. This plan enables the teacher to provide more assistance to each group individually, while the rest of the class is engaged in more independent activities.

Tip 2

If all students are engaged in an activity, they will all be working in stages on the project. If a television production is the final production, the group ready to videotape is "on stage," while the rest of the class is the audience. The rules of "Quiet on the set" and sitting quietly in seats during the taping process should be enforced. Students usually cooperate very well because they do not want to lose their opportunity to videotape when they are ready. A sign on the door indicating "Videotaping in Progress—Please Do Not Disturb!" can be very helpful!

It is helpful to design a simple "set" for use in the classroom. This can consist of a folding cardboard or wooden backdrop, upon which students can attach television news station posters or titles of television shows (such as "Book Talks" or "Health Facts"). Also, a large poster on a blank wall can be an effective background. Simple backgrounds are more effective than those with many visual distractors. A table and chairs will be necessary for certain presentations. All of this can be accomplished in a small area of the classroom, and set up just for the time when productions will be videotaped.

Tip 3

For audiotaping, students are capable of producing a tape on their own because of the simplicity of equipment. Usually, a corner of the classroom (during a quiet time), or a corner of a hall or learning center will provide the needed space and silence (the principal's office can sometimes be used for this). If the students have practiced adequately beforehand, the actual taping should not be overly time-consuming. Students will not be out of the classroom very long, and therefore will not miss much of the routine classroom activity.

Tip 4

For photography activities, the student or group of students working on a particular project can shoot pictures on their own, after instruction on the use of the camera, and after agreeing that they will not disturb other classes or students while taking photographs. If only a few students are involved at a time, the teacher can proceed with routine classroom activity.

Resources

Media Production Books for Teachers

Agnew, P., A. Kellerman, and J. Meyer. *Multimedia in the classroom.* Boston: Allyn & Bacon, 1996.

Barron, A., and G. Orwig. *New technologies for education: A beginner's guide.* Englewood, CO: Teacher Ideas Press, 1995.

Black, K. *Kidvid: Fun-damentals of video instruction.* Tucson, AZ: Zephyr Press, 1989.

Green, L. *Creative slide/tape programs.* Englewood, CO: Libraries Unlimited, 1986.

Heinich, R., M. Molenda, J. D. Russell, and S. Smaldino. *Instructional media and technologies for learning.* Englewood Cliffs, NJ: Prentice-Hall, 1996.

Kemp, J., and D. Smellie. *Planning, producing, and using instructional technologies.* New York: Harper-Collins College Publishers, 1994.

Kyker, K., and C. Curchy. *Television production for elementary and middle schools.* Englewood, CO: Libraries Unlimited, 1994.

Skill Areas Index

Audio Productions
Communication Skills, 94
Community Awareness, 90
Creative Writing, 88, 94, 96, 98
Health, 84, 86, 104, 106
Interviewing Skills, 98
Math, 88
Oral Communication, 84, 86, 88, 90, 92, 96, 98, 100, 102, 104, 106, 108, 110, 112
Reading, 92, 100
Research, 86, 90, 92, 106, 108, 112
Science, 84, 86, 104, 106
Social Studies, 84, 86, 104, 106, 112
Writing, 112
Written Communication, 90, 90, 100, 102, 106, 108

Computer Activities
Alphabetizing, 142
Averaging, 132
Creative Writing, 120
Critical Analysis, 144
Database Management, 126, 134
Drawing, 120, 136
English, 148
Estimating, 128, 132
Evaluating, 126
Goal Setting, 130
Group Awareness, 134
Group Discussion, 130
Health, 122, 144, 146
Logic, 134
Math, 128, 132
Organization, 122, 136
Proofreading, 138, 148
Reading, 126
Research, 144, 146
Science, 122, 144, 146
Self-Awareness, 134
Social Studies, 122, 144, 146
Spelling, 142
Word Processing, 122, 130, 138, 140, 142, 148
Written Communication, 136, 138, 140, 142, 144

Multimedia Productions
All Curricular Areas, 156, 166, 178
Creative Writing, 158, 162, 166
Critical Thinking, 164, 174, 176, 178, 180, 182, 184
English, 156, 158
History, 168
Interpretation and Analysis of Literature, 184
Media Analysis, 180
Narrative Writing, 184
Presentation, 160
Problem Solving, 164, 174, 176, 182
Social Studies, 168, 170
Various Curricular Areas, 172
Visual Literacy, 158, 164
Writing, 160, 170
Written Communication, 168

Photography/Transparency Activities
All Curricular Areas, 48, 50, 72, 76
Critical Thinking, 56, 64, 68, 70
Critical Viewing, 54
English, 64, 74
Group Cooperation, 58
Health, 68
History, 58
Language Arts, 74
Literature, 64
Perception, 54, 56
Research, 58
Science, 52, 60, 62, 66, 74
Social Studies, 66, 70
Visual Design, 64, 66
Visual Literacy, 54, 56

Video Productions
All Curricular Areas, 22, 34
Art, 26
Communication/Interviewing, 18
Cooperative Group Work, 14, 22, 40
Creative Writing, 26, 32
English, 12, 14, 16, 18, 20
Group Participation, 40
Health, 32
Math, 40
Oral Communication, 12, 24, 26, 30, 36, 38
Oral Presentation, 14, 16, 18, 20, 32
Point of View, 24
Reading, 12, 14, 16, 18, 24, 38
Research, 16, 20, 22, 32, 38
Science, 20, 32, 38
Social Studies, 16, 38
Spelling, 28
Writing, 38
Written Communication, 30, 36

Author/Title/Subject Index

This index lists authors, titles, and subjects from chapter 1 and the introductory sections of chapters 2–6.

Active listening, 79–80
Adams, D., 8–9
Affective domain, 2
Agnew, P., 151–52
Applying knowledge, ability to, 3–4
"Ask and Find Out" (Extracurricular activity), 80
Audio
    basic skills, 80
    productions, 79–80
Auditory messages, 5
Authorware, 152

Bell-Gredler, M. E., 3, 5
British Audiovisual Association, 7, 9, 151–52

Camera. *See* Photography
CD-ROM, 151
Cognition and curriculum: A basis for deciding what to teach, 43, 45
Cognitive domain, 2–3
Composition, 8, 44
Computer
    activities, 115–16
    literacy, 4–5, 115–16
Communication, 1, 3
"Community Multimedia Show" (extracurricular activity), 152
The conditions of learning, 2–3, 5
Considine, C., 7, 9
Content, organizing, 2–3
Copystand, 44, 204
Costa, A., 43, 45
Critical thinking. *See* Skills development
Critical viewing. *See* Viewing critically

"Developing minds," 43, 45
"Dialog Guide" (scriptwriting worksheet), 202
Digital cameras, 44

Editing, video, 204–6
"Education Week Displays" (extracurricular event), 45
Eisner, E. W., 43, 45
Environmental awareness, 1
Evaluation sheets, 189–97
Experiential involvement of learner, 1, 3, 5

Gagne, R., 2–3, 5
Gardner, H., 2, 5
Global education, 4
Guidelines, basic skills
    for audio, 80
    for photographs, 44
    for videos, 8

Haley, G., 7, 9
Hamm, M., 8–9
Hanson, J. R., 43, 45
Hearing, 79
Heinich, R., 1, 5, 43–45, 79–80, 115–16, 151–52
"Helping elementary school children learn about TV," 7, 9
"How to Spend a Million Dollars" (extracurricular activity), 116
HyperCard, 152

Individual differences, providing for, 2–3, 152
Instructional media and technologies for learning, 1, 5, 43–45, 79–80, 115–16, 151–52
Integrating technology, 1–5
Intelligence, aspects of, 3

Kellerman, A., 151–52
Kemp, J., 1, 3, 5

Lacy, L., 43, 45
Learning
    categories (Gagne), 2
    elements of, 1–2
    theories and integrating technology in the curriculum, 3
    through various senses, 7, 43, 151
Learning and instruction: Theory into practice, 3, 5
Learning styles and visual literacy: Connections and actions, 43, 45
Lehmkuhle, E., 43, 45
Lifelong learning, preparation for, 152
Lighting, 8, 44
LinkWay, 152
Listening skills, 79
LOGO computer language, 115

Macro lens, 204
Media, five useful, 152. *See also* Multimedia
Meyer, J., 151–52
"Million Dollars, How to Spend," (extracurricular activity), 116
Mindstorms: Children, computers, and powerful ideas, 115–16
Molenda, M., 1, 5, 43–45, 79–80, 115–16, 151–52
Motivating students, 2–3
    putting excitement back in learning, 8
Multimedia
    presentation tools, 152
    productions, 151–52
    selection of media, 151–52
Multimedia in the classroom, 151–52
Multiple intelligences: The theory and practice, 2, 5

Objectives-based learning, 2–3

Papert, S., 115–16
Participatory learning, 2–4
Perception, 1, 3
Perelman, L. J., 115–16
Photography, 43–45
    in the classroom, 44
    guidelines, 44
Planning, involving students in, 5
Planning, producing, and using instructional technologies, 1, 3, 5
Portfolio assessment, 8
Psychomotor domain, 2

Relevance of learning, 2
Report of the British Audiovisual Association, 7, 9, 151–52
Right brain processes, versus left brain, 43
"Rule of thirds," 8, 44
Russell, J. D., 1, 5, 43–45, 79–80, 115–16, 151–52

Saxton, B., 8–9
School's out: A radical new formula for the revitalization of America's educational system, 115–16
"Script Guide Sheet" (scriptwriting worksheet), 203
"Scriptwriting Guidelines" (scriptwriting worksheet), 201
Silver, H. F., 43, 45
Singer, D., 7, 9
Singer, J., 7, 9
Skills, production. *See* Guidelines, basic skills

Skills development
    analysis, 8
    communication, 1, 5
    cooperation, 5
    critical thinking, 7–8, 151
Slides, 151, 152
Smaldino, S., 1, 5, 43–45, 79–80, 115–16, 151–52
Smellie, D., 1, 3, 5
Sound effects, 80
Special effects, 8
Spoehr, K., 43, 45
Spreadsheet (computer program), 116
Strong, R. W., 43, 45
Student-produced visuals, 8, 44. *See also* Visuals
    showcasing, 9, 45, 152

Tape recorder, 79–80
Teachers
    changing roles of, 116
    effectiveness of, 2
"Teaching students critical viewing skills," 8–9
Technological productions, rationale for classroom use, 1
Television, 4
    and critical viewing, 7–8
    production skills, 8
Thinking skills, higher-level, 4. *See also* Skills development
"Thinking skills and visual literacy," 43, 45
Transparencies. *See* Photography

"VCR visual techniques for fifth- and sixth-graders— More than turning it on!," 8–9
Video
    editing, 204–6
    productions, 7–9
"Video Night" (extracurricular event), 9
Videodisc, 151
Viewing critically, 7–8, 152
Visual competency, 8
Visual information processing, 43, 45
Visual literacy, 4, 43
Visual messages: Integrating imagery into instruction, 7, 9
Visuals
    and learning, 43–44
    in multimedia, 152
    student-produced, 8–9, 43–44, 152

Zuckerman, D., 7, 9

Resources *from* Libraries Unlimited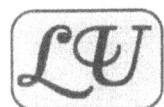

THE INTERNET RESOURCE DIRECTORY FOR K–12 TEACHERS AND LIBRARIANS
Elizabeth B. Miller

This award-winning annual offers you access to current and accurate information on the most useful and reliable Web sites on the Internet. Designed for educators, it organizes material by curriculum areas. Sites are annotated and screened, and this edition has increased emphasis on sites with lesson plans. FREE UPDATES listed at www.lu.com/Internet_Resource_Directory. **All levels**.
Please call for information on our most current edition.

THE INTERNET AND INSTRUCTION
Activities and Ideas
2d Edition
Ann E. Barron and Karen S. Ivers

Surfing the Net in the classroom? It's easy! This guide provides relevant, feasible, and detailed ideas and activities. Expanded coverage of cross-curricular activities makes this new edition so thorough, that it works as a text as well as a supplement. **Grades 4–12**.
xi, 244p. 8½x11 paper ISBN 1-56308-613-1

WADING THE WORLD WIDE WEB
Internet Activities for Beginners
Keith Kyker

Give your students confidence-building, entry-level Internet experience, to encourage them to fully explore each Web page they visit. All projects include step-by-step instructions and 10 to 15 related questions. **Grades 3 and up**.
xvii, 170p. 8½x11 paper ISBN 1-56308-605-0

NEW TECHNOLOGIES FOR EDUCATION
A Beginner's Guide
3rd Edition
Ann E. Barron and Gary W. Orwig

This updated version of the highly popular book looks at the technologies impacting education, including school LANs, the Internet, and multimedia. Deepen your "tech" knowledge with this overview of compact disc technologies, videodiscs, digital audio, digitized video, telecommunications, and hypermedia. An excellent resource for all educators!
xv, 295p. 8½x11 paper ISBN 1-56308-477-5

DECISION POINTS
Boolean Logic for Computer Users and Beginning Online Searchers
Janaye M. Houghton and Robert S. Houghton

Help students make astute online searching decisions to get them quickly to the facts they need. This activity guide, full of reproducible worksheets, teaches strategies that carry over into more logical thinking offline too. A must buy for classroom and computer teachers and school librarians! **Grades 5–12**.
viii, 155p. 8½x11 paper ISBN 1-56308-672-7

For a FREE catalog or to place an order, please contact:

Libraries Unlimited/Teacher Ideas Press
Dept. B996 · P.O. Box 6633 · Englewood, CO 80155-6633
1-800-237-6124, ext. 1 · Fax: 303-220-8843 · E-mail: lu-books@lu.com

Check out our Web site!
www.lu.com

www.ingramcontent.com/pod-product-compliance
Lightning Source LLC
Chambersburg PA
CBHW060249240426
43673CB00047B/1899